TENNYSON: IN MEMORIAM

by
K. W. GRANSDEN

EDWARD ARNOLD

© K. W. GRANSDEN 1964

First published 1964
by Edward Arnold (Publishers) Ltd.,
41 Maddox Street, London, W1R 0AN

Reprinted 1971

Printed in Great Britain by
The Camelot Press Ltd., London and Southampton

General Preface

It has become increasingly clear in recent years that what both the advanced six-former and the university student need most by way of help in their literary studies are close critical analyses and evaluations of individual works. Generalisations about periods or authors, general chat about the Augustan Age or the Romantic Movement, have their uses; but often they provide merely the illusion of knowledge and understanding of literature. All too often students come up to the university under the impression that what is required of them in their English literature courses is the referring of particular works to the appropriate generalisations about the writer or his period. Without taking up the anti-historical position of some of the American 'New Critics', we can nevertheless recognise the need for critical studies that concentrate on the work of literary art rather than on its historical background or cultural environment.

The present series is therefore designed to provide studies of individual plays, novels and groups of poems and essays, which are known to be widely studied in sixth forms and in universities. The emphasis is on clarification and evaluation; biographical and historical facts, while they may of course be referred to as helpful to an understanding of particular elements in a writer's work, will be subordinated to critical discussion. What kind of work is this? What exactly goes on here? How good is this work and why? These are the questions which each writer will try to answer.

DAVID DAICHES

Acknowledgements

I am grateful to Dr. Catherine Ing, Fellow of St. Hilda's College and University Lecturer in English Literature at Oxford, for reading this book in manuscript and making a number of valuable suggestions and corrections. I should also like to thank my wife for her help in clarifying a number of obscurities.

K. W. G.

Contents

1. The Poet and the Age

Tennyson's poetic career extends from 1830 until his death in 1892. It was a time of religious, political and social change, but of change (generally) towards stability. Continental Europe gradually emerged from the upheavals which, a generation earlier, had aroused the English romantics to a fervour of revolutionary idealism and had seemed to justify all the enlightened eighteenth-century radicalism they had inherited. In England, the Reform riots in the early 1830s brought the country to the edge of civil war—more than fifty years later (in the poem addressed to Mary Boyle) Tennyson recalls how he had helped to put out rick fires when 'lowly minds were madden'd to the height by tonguester tricks'—but the established order, though challenged, remained, adapting itself where necessary to new pressures; and England settled down to a peace broken only by the brief, fiercely patriotic Crimean War, described by Trevelyan as 'merely a foolish expedition, made for no sufficient reason, because the English people were bored by peace'. The bitterest intellectual battles of mid-Victorian England were fought not over political issues but over religious ones. It seemed to some that the biological and geological discoveries of the evolutionists shed a new and doubtful light on man's origin, his role in the universe and his future.

Of all these complexities Tennyson is the most sensitive and representative poet. But despite the persistence with which he explored the difficult issues of his time, despite his spectacular innovatory power over language, he remained by temperament a conservative and a traditionalist. New ideas interested him not so much for their own sake as for the light they threw on his own mental processes and, through these, on the mind of man and his place in the universe. Thus he stands in a great tradition of enquiry stretching from the seventeenth century, through the eighteenth, to Wordsworth. The very emotion he has received most praise for rendering, that of melancholy (see Mr. T. S. Eliot's essay on *In Memoriam*) was itself a characteristic theme of English poets up to and including Wordsworth, as was the idealism with which he sought to oppose the bigotry, the materialism and the self-interest of his age.

Before trying to show how Tennyson innovated, what he added to tradition, I must show to what extent he leaned on tradition. Compare the following passages:

> Heaven from all creatures hides the book of fate,
> All but the page prescribed, their present state.
> From brutes what men, from men what spirits know,
> Or who could suffer being here below?
> The lamb thy riot dooms to bleed today,
> Had he thy reason, would be skip and play?
> Pleased to the last, he crops the flowery food,
> And licks the hand just raised to shed his blood.
> Oh blindness to the future! kindly given
> That each may fill the circle mark'd by heaven. . . .
> Hope humbly then; with trembling pinions soar;
> Wait the great teacher, Death, and God adore.
> What future bliss, he gives thee not to know,
> But gives that hope to be thy blessing now.
> Hope springs eternal in the human breast:
> Man never Is, but always To be blest.
> The soul uneasy and confined from home,
> Rests and expatiates in a life to come.
>
> . . . The lamb rejoiceth in the year,
> And raceth freely with his fere,
> And answers to his mother's calls
> From the flower'd furrow. In a time
> Of which he wots not, run short pains
> Thro' his warm heart; and then, from whence
> He knows not, on his light there falls
> A shadow; and his native slope,
> Where he was wont to leap and climb,
> Floats from his sick and filmed eyes,
> And something in the darkness draws
> His forehead earthward, and he dies.
> Shall man live thus in joy and hope
> As a young lamb who cannot dream,
> Living, but that he shall live on?
> Shall we not look into the laws
> Of life and death, and things that seem,
> And things that be, and analyse
> Our double nature, and compare

All creeds till we have found the one,
If one there be?

The first of those passages is from Pope's *Essay on Man*, the second from Tennyson's early poem, 'Supposed Confessions of a Second-Rate Sensitive Mind'. The problem, it may be said, has not changed—to try to understand what Pope called 'the immense design'; but it has become harder to solve. Yet for all his air of moral confidence, his sensible acceptance of the human condition, Pope does not entirely repress those qualifying reservations so typical of Tennyson's own speculative essays: particularly in the closing lines of the passage quoted, where the uneasiness, strangeness and limitations of human life are admitted and where the soul expatiating in a life to come may recall Tennyson's 'from state to state the spirit walks' (*In Memoriam* LXXXII). And the largeness of Pope's vision depended, no less than Tennyson's, on being 'slave to no sect'. Thus Tennyson's analyses explore familiar ground, but with a new and sharper sense of alienation, a temperamental tendency towards doubt and despair strengthened by new evidence which, it seemed, had further undermined the old confidence. Yet it is that old confidence, enriched by the visionary power Wordsworth brought into poetry, which Tennyson throughout his career was always trying to recover. This, 'the first, last purpose of the human soul', remained his central purpose, and he was too serious an artist to let himself be deflected by the sheer novelty-value of nineteenth-century theories and discoveries.

In some ways, then, Tennyson was closer to Pope and Gray than to, say, Browning. The emotional intimacies of *In Memoriam* may cause us to overlook the way in which its highly polished quatrains can encompass the epigrammatic—

> The world which credits what is done
> Is cold to all that might have been—

and the formal. There is an eighteenth-century decorum, for instance, in LXIV with its classical abstractions, its balanced, conventional epithets, its repeated, generalising use of the definite article:

> Who breaks his birth's invidious bar
> And grasps the skirts of happy chance,
> And breasts the blows of circumstance,
> And grapples with his evil star;

Who makes by force his merit known
  And lives to clutch the golden keys,
  To mould a mighty state's decrees,
  And shape the whisper of the throne;

And moving up from high to higher,
  Becomes on Fortune's crowning slope
  The pillar of a people's hope,
  The centre of a world's desire.

Tennyson was by temperament and inclination a quietist in a strenuous
age, a classical scholar, a fastidious stylist and an introvert in what he
called 'the new dark ages of the popular press', when the ideas of the
élite were diluted for a new urban middle-class reading public which he
felt to be lacking in mental stamina and discipline and easily imposed
on by idea-mongers:

For their knowing and know-nothing books are
  scatter'd from hand to hand.

Tennyson's own refusals to simplify the complex led to the kind of
ambiguities in his own work which some modern critics have wrongly
supposed to be the result of his own inadequate understanding (an error
into which no Victorian critic fell). In fact, everything seemed much
more difficult to him than it had to, say, Shelley. It was all very well for
Shelley to launch, in *Queen Mab*, a rhapsodical and rapturous attack on
tyranny and venality and to offer a vision of heaven on earth and earth
in heaven

where care and sorrow, impotence and crime,
  languor, disease and ignorance dare not come
  . . . where friends and lovers meet to part no more.

Shelley's verse, glittering and impatient, out-soars human objections
and delays: its ardours excited undergraduates of Tennyson's generation,
including Tennyson himself; but he soon found himself temperamentally
unwilling to assent to its speed and tone. With many of its beliefs he
agreed, as for instance he would have agreed with Shelley's assertion
that 'the destiny of man can scarcely be so degraded that he was born
only to die': he says the same thing in *In Memoriam*. But when Shelley
rushes on to say that 'if such should be the case, delusions, especially the
gross and preposterous one of the existing religion, can scarcely be

supposed to exalt it', Tennyson would have felt that Shelley was rushing things, taking for granted propositions which needed much more examination than revolutionary idealism was prepared to undertake; he would have felt a lack of respect for traditional values, or of what he would have called reverence: by which he meant a pausing before experience and its consequences, a recognition of the validity of doubt and despair and of the need to fight and conquer them, not to sweep them aside as irrelevant. The nineteenth century, with its scientific advances, the gradual spread of enlightenment, suggested a whole new set of tough facts to be digested and incorporated into experience. Much of what the romantics had rough-hewn Tennyson had to refine, probe and modify: in him a visionary passion hardly less intense than Shelley's and hardly less self-centred than Wordsworth's was balanced and checked by a pragmatism, a cautious slowing down of response, a suspension of enthusiasm (which, Valéry remarked, is not an artist's state of mind).

Tennyson had the artist's and scientist's passion for documentation and research: he lacked and distrusted the passion of the revolutionary for creating and imposing exclusive ideas of truth by skipping inconvenient evidence. He was by nature drawn rather to the Coleridgean aim of synthesising the positive truths of religion and philosophy. Nor did he have any illusions about human nature. Thus one of his best known poems, 'The Higher Pantheism', in which he may be held to have summed up his philosophy of life, is remarkable not so much for the all-embracing splendour of its world picture as for its account of man's alienation from creation. Man's soul has made him the only being capable of comprehending and describing creation; but the perverseness of his will, his self-destructiveness, also make him the only being capable of spoiling this perfection. 'Dark is the world to thee': yet it is only through man's fragmented vision that the splendour of the universe is even glimpsed. And it is man's fate (his 'doom') to bring about this fragmentation. Behind the poem, as behind so much of Tennyson's work, lies the shadow of an older wisdom than evolution: the Fall.

Although Tennyson attacked the evils of his time, especially money-worship (there is a personal bitterness in *Maud* and 'Locksley Hall' which reminds us that he himself in his early years had suffered through being poor and uninfluential) his attacks are more those of a moralist than of a 'committed' radical reformer. It is clear from 'Aylmer's Field' that he felt it to be the duty of the English ruling class to maintain the traditional virtues of the established order at a time when heads were rolling in France: the poem is a historical one set in the late eighteenth century but the moral is one which Tennyson upheld for his own time: that the ruling class must show spiritual insight, flexibility, and common sense if they are not to drag England down with them: 'was this a time for them to flaunt their pride?' He felt that without sympathy and humility nothing worth while would be handed on to the next generation. The ironic ending of 'Aylmer's Field' is significant: the parents' pride and misguidedness not only destroys their daughter but their house; the land reverts to nature and one more achievement of stability and order is lost because of human complacency and inflexibility.

Tennyson's attitude to progress (often misunderstood) was a very long-term one. He says at the end of *The Princess*:

> This fine old world of ours is but a child
> Yet in the go-cart. Patience! Give it time
> To learn its limbs: there is a hand that guides.

And in a late poem, 'The Play', he says:

> Act first, this Earth, a stage so gloom'd with woe,
>   You all but sicken at the shifting scenes.
> And yet be patient. Our Playwright may show
>   In some fifth Act what this wild Drama means.

The words 'may' and 'some' are characteristic qualifying words. Even the most hopeful prognosis is tentative and not to be verified in his own lifetime or that of his age. Consequently patience was necessary: this is perhaps the chief moral lesson of *In Memoriam*. And the line 'you all but sicken at the shifting scenes' illustrates Tennyson's lack of natural sympathy for the reforming spirit, his tendency to shrink away from the dirty work of life into a more congenial contemplation of man's spiritual potentialities.

Tennyson led an uneventful, even an indolent, life. After the hostile reception that greeted his first two books (the 1830 and 1832 volumes which included the 'Supposed Confessions of a Second-Rate Sensitive Mind not in Unity with itself', the two Marianas, 'The Lotos Eaters', and 'The Palace of Art') he relapsed into himself, passive, brooding, drifting, pursuing his own inspiration or inner vision, his 'gleam'. As he tells us in 'Audley Court'

> —having wherewithal,
> And in the fallow leisure of my life
> A rolling stone of here and everywhere,
> Did what I would—

he continued writing, in the words of James Spedding, 'like a crocodile, sideways and onward'. In 1833 his closest friend and Cambridge contemporary Arthur Hallam died in Vienna at the age of twenty-two. Intensely affected by this as by no previous and by no subsequent experience in his life, Tennyson began writing a series of elegies which were eventually published in 1850 (the year of his marriage and elevation to the laureateship) as *In Memoriam*, his greatest poem (and the greatest long poem in English between *The Prelude* and *The Waste Land*).

Yet although *In Memoriam* is Tennyson's central work it cannot be read in isolation. Much led up to it.

> Dreaming, she knew it was a dream:
> She felt he was and was not there.
> She woke: the babble of the stream
> Fell, and, without, the steady glare
> Shrank one sick willow sere and small.
> The river-bed was dusty-white;
> And all the furnace of the light
> Struck up against the blinding wall.

There can be no mistaking the novelty here, or the power. This is not the sensuousness of Milton or Keats but a passionate, even a violent exoticism. In a number of his early poems Tennyson is like some English landscape painter exposed to the harsh glare of Mediterranean light; he experiments with more dramatic effects than he could find at home. His fascination with this kind of imagery remained throughout his life, as a temptation deeply felt though constantly resisted ('better fifty years of Europe than a cycle of Cathay'). In *In Memoriam* it has no place, though it perhaps survives in remote geological speculation:

> There rolls the deep where grew the tree.
> O earth, what changes hast thou seen!
> There where the long street roars, hath been
> The stillness of the central sea.

But the pull in Tennyson away from the civilised, the homely, was strong, almost Baudelairian, though he repressed it. It finds expression in, for instance, the lines 'To Ulysses' (F. T. Palgrave's brother Gifford) or the lines beginning 'You ask me why, tho' ill at ease', an early poem expressing a qualified satisfaction with England and a desire (never fulfilled, except for a couple of visits to Spain and Portugal) to see 'the palms and temples of the south'. Tennyson in this poem weighs up English institutions, 'settled government' and the fact that 'a man may speak the thing he will', against this desire to escape. In the lines to Palgrave, written much later (in 1888) he professes himself satisfied with the Isle of Wight; but the longing for strange skies was never entirely exorcised. It symbolises for him the 'bursting of all links of habit', escape from moral strain and from the disappointments and frustrations of Victorian England, as in the famous lines in 'Locksley Hall':

Never come the trader, never floats an European flag,
Slides the bird o'er lustrous woodland, swings the trailer from the crag;

Droops the heavy-blossomed bower, hangs the heavy-fruited tree,
Summer isles of Eden lying in dark-purple spheres of sea.

There methinks would be enjoyment more than in this march of mind,
In the steamship, in the railway, in the thoughts that shake mankind.

There the passions cramp'd no longer shall have scope and breathing
    space;
I will take some savage woman, she shall rear my dusky race.

The charm and eloquence of these lines is not destroyed by the prompt rejection of them which follows, the recall to stern reality, the characteristic dismissive labelling of them as 'again the dream, the fancy'. This veering between dreams and reality is typical of Tennyson. As he grew older, his criticisms of English society continued to erupt like the grumblings of a volcano thought extinct; while his attachment to the English landscape grew deeper. One can trace this through *Maud* to the second 'Locksley Hall' with attacks on demagogy and commercialism; and in his old age he told Carlyle 'I should like to get away from all this tumult and turmoil of civilisation and live on the top of a tropical mountain'. Thus Tennyson was on the one hand escapist, lotos-eater and dreamer; and on the other the responsible laureate, husband and father, sweeping the paths at Farringford on autumn afternoons.

Although there are important visionary elements in it, *In Memoriam* must be read primarily as a domestic poem. The metre is domestic, conversational, at times almost demure (though it can rise to grandeur)— the delayed rhyme helps here. Much of the imagery is drawn from domestic life. The poem offers no escape from the slow living-through of experience which it represents.

Had Hallam lived he would have married Tennyson's sister Emily; while the marriage of another sister, Cecilia, to another friend, Edmund Lushington, is celebrated in the epilogue. A strong family sense informs the poem, e.g. in LX, in which the poet's spirit, after losing Hallam, is compared to 'some poor girl whose heart is set on one whose rank exceeds her own'; and in XCVII, in which the dead man, with his new knowledge, is compared to a husband, preoccupied with 'a thousand things' while Tennyson sees himself as the meek wife content to serve her master. Elsewhere Tennyson writes of his 'widowed heart' and of the 'household jar' (for he could be irritated as well as pleased by domestic routine) which gets in the way of contemplation. Again, in XX, the poet's griefs are compared to children in a household where the father has died (not to servants, as Bradley says):

> But open converse is there none,
>   So much the vital spirits sink
>   To see the vacant chair, and think
> 'How good! how kind! and he is gone'.

There are also the gardening images in LXXXI and LXXXII.

By choosing to stay put, by growing into England, Tennyson found himself a critic of some aspects of his age. One is less aware of this in *In Memoriam* than in some of the other poems; though by publishing the poem at all he was prepared for the criticism that in an age of great public issues he had chosen to turn aside to 'private sorrow's barren song' (see XXI); but he does not argue about this, and it is clear that at this central point of his creative career public matters were unimportant to him, his concern being at once with more personal and with larger issues, transcending local frontiers and involving the future of mankind itself. There is a synthesis of private and national responses in *Maud*, but this poem is a special case: the elements of its plot—the rich father, the poor lover, the arranged marriage, the atmosphere of political and economic corruption—seem to have had a special significance for Tennyson; while the feverish conclusion, with its recruiting-poster rhetoric, is naturally linked to the start of the Crimean War. The poem's opening and closing sections, in which private memories are mixed with angry criticism, are written in a long, nervous, rapid metre based on the rhythm of the trochee or dactyl; the large number of unstressed syllables helps to speed up the bitterness and indignation. Other poems relevant here are the two 'Locksley Halls', 'Rizpah', 'Vastness' and 'Despair'. There is a marked contrast of tempo between these poems and the slower, quieter movement of *In Memoriam* and the great blank verse poems like 'Ulysses', 'Tithonus', and the *Idylls*. 'Rizpah' and 'Despair' should be read for the violence of their disgust at the commercialism of the age and for their defiant compassion towards the victim of a society in which the evolutionary principle of the survival of the fittest seemed to operate in economic and social spheres as well as in nature. In 'Vastness' we find a recollection of the central theme of *In Memoriam*:

> What is it all, if we all of us end
>   but in being our own corpse-coffins at last,
> Swallowed in Vastness, lost in Silence,
>   drown'd in the deeps of a meaningless Past?
>
> What but a murmur of gnats in the gloom, or a
>   moment's anger of bees in their hive?—
>
>   *   *   *   *   *
>
> Peace, let it be! for I loved him and love him
>   for ever: the dead are not dead but alive.

Earlier in the poem, we find political as well as metaphysical rhetoric:

> Lies upon this side, lies upon that side, truthless
>   violence mourn'd by the Wise,
> Thousands of voices drowning his own in a
>   popular torrent of lies upon lies.

(The word 'popular' in Tennyson is usually a word of scorn). We are in the mood of the second 'Locksley Hall': the *laudator temporis acti*, the man of naturally aristocratic temper launching out against the 'common deluge', lamenting the decadence of all he values—'poor old Heraldry, poor old History, poor old Poetry passing hence, in the common deluge drowning old political common-sense'. One notes the inclusion of heraldry, the art with which the people have least to do; the characteristic repetition of 'common' in a good sense after it has been used in a bad one; and the opposition of a traditional Tory pragmatism to the revolutionary radicalism which seemed to be threatening all the old values.

There are only two sections of *In Memoriam* which have this explicit political and social concern. One is the famous new year poem CVI ('Ring out the narrowing lust of gold'); the other is CXXVII, in which Tennyson looks beyond the crises of the age and hears

> A deeper voice across the storm
>
> Proclaiming social truth shall spread,
>   And justice, ev'n tho' thrice again
>   The red fool-fury of the Seine
> Should pile her barricades with dead . . .

'The red fool-fury of the Seine' shares the same adjective with Nature 'red in tooth and claw' and underlines Tennyson's feeling that force without morality, whether in the macrocosm or the microcosm, is merely destructive.

On the whole Tennyson the prophet, like Tennyson the moral teacher and castigator of his age, has not been well received by modern critics, who have tended to reject the poems in which he is responding to his age in order to anthologise him 'for all time' as the author of, say, twenty beautiful and 'timeless' lyrics and natural descriptions. I do not think Tennyson can be treated in this way. To do so is to reduce his stature as the central poet of one of the great centuries of English history and to turn him into a sort of superior Dowson, a fragmentary and legendary poet whose work has no links with its age or, where it has such links, is bad.

It is sometimes forgotten that Tennyson was respected by the best minds of the day as well as by the thousands of middle-class pilgrims who finally drove him from Farringford. Not only poets and writers but statesmen, historians, theologians and dons visited him and regarded him as their equal and even as their superior. He was co-founder and first president of the Metaphysical Society which included among its members Bagehot, Gladstone, Froude, Manning, Martineau, Huxley, Mark Pattison, Ruskin and Sidgwick. Martineau praised the 'dissolving influence' of Tennyson's verse on the society's dogmatic discussions. (The society eventually died because, as Tennyson said with characteristic humour, 'after ten years of strenuous effort no one had succeeded in even defining the term metaphysics'). Thus Tennyson retained throughout his life the intellectual primacy he had established, for all his shambling inarticulateness, when as an undergraduate he became a somewhat unsatisfactory member of the earnest, transcendentalist Cambridge society known as the 'Apostles'. He was an intellectual and a spokesman for intellectuals in a way no other writer with his huge popularity ever was. Even the poet of the successful middle years does not quite occlude the aloof, drifting figure of the 1830s and 40s, the aristocratic bohemian, the Lincolnshire scholar-gypsy lost in a contemplative cloud of tobacco smoke. For all its didacticism, his writing is always emotionally honest; and much of the difficulty in his work comes from his continual attempts to offer, without falsifying the evidence, a vision of life which in its grandeur and nobility tried to rise above the materialism, whether scientific or economic, of his age. Consequently his best work was always liable to be misunderstood by people less honest than himself. I think there is still some misunderstanding, not only about *In Memoriam* but about the *Idylls of the King*, the principal achievement of Tennyson's middle years. The *Idylls* are beyond the scope of this essay, but they are the English epic which Milton nearly wrote, so it is curious that some modern critics have written them off as pot-boilers. Their theme is, ultimately, the same as that of *In Memoriam*: the courage and vision of man; they seek in mythology a pattern which *In Memoriam* finds in personal experience. In their greatest passages they are transcendental, that is, they look beyond the 'feeble twilight of this world' to 'that other where we see as we are seen', and where vision becomes reality and the apparently real phenomenal world becomes unimportant, as in the closing lines of 'The Holy Grail' where it is stated that after the King's earthly work is done he may then surrender himself to transcendental experience until

> this earth he walks on seems not earth,
> This light that strikes his eyeball is not light,
> This air that smites his forehead is not air
> But vision—yea, his very hand and foot—
> In moments when he feels he cannot die. . . .

So too the steady grandeur of Arthur's lament before his passing, his fear lest man lose this vision—

> I found Him in the shining of the stars,
> I mark'd Him in the flowering of His fields,
> But in His ways with men I found Him not.

is very much in the mood of *In Memoriam*. Compare CXXIV:

> I found Him not in world or sun
>   Or insect's wing or eagle's eye;
>   Nor thro' the questions men may try,
> The petty cobwebs we have spun.

There is no contradiction here. God is manifest in nature; it is man who is blind. Looking for God through telescopes or microscopes is trying to reduce his grandeur to the limits of earthly knowledge. Later in his speech Arthur says that we cannot see the beauty of God's world and purpose 'perchance because we see not to the close'. The word 'close' recurs in the last two lines of *In Memoriam* where it suggests both 'the closing cycle' when God in man will be fully revealed, and also the closing or coming together of two people in love: thus beautifully bringing into unison the two principal themes of the poem.

> Until we close with all we loved
> And all we flow from, soul in soul.

We may also compare the end of *In Memoriam* CXXVIII (where the qualifying 'in part' corresponds to Arthur's 'perchance'):

> I see in part
> That all, as in some piece of art,
> Is toil coöperant to an end.

The most important characteristic of Tennyson's poetic thinking is his need to submit all ideas to the test of his own feelings and his own vision. It is this which make his philosophical poetry so much more than the versified doctrine it is sometimes taken to be. Thus, in *In Memoriam* CXVIII, his moral passion, and the grandeur of his imagery, transmute what might have been a crude Wellsian outline of history chapter into something noble and far-reaching:

> They say,
> The solid earth whereon we tread

In tracts of fluent heat began,
　　And grew to seeming-random forms,
　　The seeming prey of cyclic storms,
Till at the last arose the man;

Who throve and branch'd from clime to clime,
　　The herald of a higher race,
　　And of himself in higher place,
If so he type this work of time

Within himself, from more to more;
　　Or, crown'd with attributes of woe
　　Like glories, move his course, and show
That life is not as idle ore,

But iron dug from central gloom,
　　And heated hot with burning fears,
　　And dipt in baths of hissing tears,
And batter'd with the shocks of doom

To shape and use. Arise and fly
　　The reeling Faun, the sensual feast;
　　Move upward, working out the beast,
And let the ape and tiger die.

In this poem, by repeating the word 'seeming' Tennyson introduces into his account of evolving creation a sense of divine (if hidden) purpose; while the twice repeated definite article in 'till at the last arose the man' brings grandeur and a sense of moral climax into the development of man which biologically was gradual (and Tennyson says nothing to contradict this). We then move on from the evolution of the universe to the possibility of man's copying the sequence in his own development, both on earth, generation by generation, and in heaven, where the dead individual will be shown (see LXXXV)

　　　　All knowledge that the sons of flesh
　　　Shall gather in the cycled times.

Tennyson's ideas on relative and absolute knowledge before and after death can to some extent be related to traditional ideas on the subject. Thus Donne, addressing the dead Elizabeth Drury in his *Second Anniversary*, says 'In heaven thou strait knowst all'. The difference in the two views is that Tennyson thought that this 'all' would be revealed, not only to the dead instantly (as in Donne) but to the living gradually, as the race developed. Donne thought of man as always likely to be more or less ignorant: yet he seems almost to play into Tennyson's hands when he writes

> Why grasse is green, or why our blood is red,
> Are mysteries that none have reach'd unto.

This of course is exactly the kind of knowledge that man on earth was, by Tennyson's time, discovering: it is as though all knowledge is stored up in heaven, with so much doled out to each generation. Donne, of course, seems to dismiss such knowledge as in any case mere pedantry, to be revealed in heaven if important and, if not, at once forgotten: 'an hundred controversies of an ant'. Here Donne harks back to the *contemptus mundi* of the Middle Ages. Tennyson lived at a time which took such knowledge seriously enough to make considerable additions to it; so the problem was to work these advances into metaphysics without belittling either the advances or the metaphysics. It might even have seemed to a Victorian that to die young was to be cheated of one's share in an unprecedented intellectual advance.

> So many worlds, so much to do,
> So little done, such things to be

Those well-known lines exactly convey the sense of intellectual excitement of that time, together with its realisation that man was still only at the beginning. Consequently, it would be no use for man to put his trust wholly in knowledge while knowledge remained, for all its advances, still imperfect. So Tennyson introduced wisdom or reverence as concepts complementary to knowledge. The contrast between the two, which occurs in *In Memoriam*, seems first to have been made in the stanzas (written in the metre of *In Memoriam*) 'Love thou thy land':

> Make knowledge circle with the winds,
> But let her herald, Reverence, fly
> Before her to whatever sky
> Bear seed of men and growth of minds.

Compare the introduction to *In Memoriam*:

> Let knowledge grow from more to more
> But more of reverence in us dwell:

and CXIV:

> I would the great world grew like thee,
>> Who grewest not alone in power
>> And knowledge, but by year and hour
> In reverence and in charity.

It is in that section of *In Memoriam* that knowledge is also contrasted with wisdom:

> For she is earthly of the mind,
>> But Wisdom heavenly of the soul.

Wisdom and reverence seem to have meant to Tennyson an acknowledgement of the divine purpose of creation not yet revealed by knowledge; a matter of patience, experience and spiritual insight born of humility. This must be the meaning of the words 'knowledge comes, but wisdom lingers' in 'Locksley Hall', and of the following lines in the poem 'Love and Duty':

> wait, and love himself will bring
> The drooping flower of knowledge chang'd to fruit
> Of wisdom.

Again, in the late poem 'The Ancient Sage', Tennyson writes

> For knowledge is the swallow on the lake
> That sees and stirs the surface-shadow there,
> But never yet has dipt into the abysm.

In *In Memoriam* Tennyson dips into the abysm; so too, King Arthur's magic sword comes from the depths of the lake and, like the Rhinegold, returns to the depths when the cycle is accomplished and the work done. Until the time comes when knowledge is perfect, when (in Browning's words) 'earth has attained to heaven', wisdom alone can give man the spiritual insight which is his supreme achievement.

We may now return to *In Memoriam* CXVIII. Tennyson has conducted us from the world of natural to the world of moral science, tying up the two in the last line of the poem, where the ape and tiger are not only earlier and cruder species in evolution which may one day be superseded like the mastodon, but are also the beast in man which must be conquered. The metal-working imagery of the last stanzas of the poem seems appropriate because we have been talking about the earth being formed out of cooling matter, but in fact introduces a new, though related, idea. Man, if he 'move his course' (and this implies moral effort, since by this stage man is no longer at the mercy of chance and circumstance, and may improve if he wishes) can show that human life is not useless matter but something made valuable by exposure to experience. The central gloom is not only local, in the image, but is also the dark origin of life. Thus all that 'they say' about the origin of species can be fitted into a feeling of hope as to what lies ahead. The visionary quality of Tennyson's metabiology seems at times to anticipate the creative evolutionists of fifty years later; not only in this poem but in the lines about true marriage in *The Princess*:

> Purpose in purpose, will in will, they grow,
> The single pure and perfect animal,
> The two-cell'd heart beating, with one full stroke,
> Life.

It seems clear that we have to deal here with something more interesting than a mind adrift amid the catchwords of Victorian scientific theory. Tennyson is really following out Wordsworth's prediction that the poet must 'carry sensation into the midst of the objects of the Science itself' and 'lend his divine spirit to the transfiguration' of science into 'a form of flesh and blood'. Moreover, he performed this task as a pioneer, publishing *In Memoriam* nine years before the appearance of *The Origin of Species*. Of course, evolutionary ideas had been formulated long before Darwin collected and presented the evidence for natural selection, and Tennyson was drawing on such forerunners as Herschel and Lyell to furnish a whole new imagery, a new framework of terminology: so the psychological and social sciences furnished Mr. W. H. Auden with a new imagery in the 1930s. (It was Freud who said that all his discoveries had long been known to artists, and it is a major function of the poet to put into currency the bare technical thinking of his time, to 'enrich the blood of the world'.)

All speculation about man's future potential both as a member of a race which is part of the evolutionary process and as an individual, must remain hypothetical—if one likes, wishful thinking. Tennyson admits this in *In Memoriam* LV—

> The wish that of the living whole
> No life may fail beyond the grave

—but argues that this wish may correspond to (derive from) our divine intuitions ('what we have the likest God within the soul'). Tennyson faced the task of reconciling materialist theories about the past history of the universe (suns, gases, primitive cells and so on) with moral theory (man as a being capable of creating unique spiritual values). 'And thoughts of men are widen'd with the process of the suns'. No theory can do more than predict the course events may take: evolutionary theory itself showed that at various stages in the development of life a number of choices and directions were open. So man might stay as he was; or improve; or deteriorate. His long climb from the ape pointed strongly to improvement, and Victorian advances would also have suggested a meliorist hypothesis as reasonable. Any writer who adopts such a hypothesis risks being dismissed as utopian, just as any writer who predicts that man will deterioriate tends to be written off as sick (e.g. Orwell in *1984*). The third possibility, that man would stay as he was, would have seemed to be flying in the face of history as the Victorians saw it.)

In his moments of hope and faith Tennyson felt that man would improve morally: for once it is granted that man has spiritual qualities denied to the rest of the universe, qualities whose appearance marked a new stage in the evolution of life (a stage not required by the concept of natural selection and the survival of the fittest), it may reasonably follow that man is capable of improving these qualities. In his moments of doubt and despair, Tennyson was daunted by the possibility that man, if he *had* arisen wholly through the blind operation of natural selection, might be doomed to die as were his remote ancestors and all his precious differentiating moral qualities be a mere cruel joke of nature's. This kind of uncertainty as to which way man will go is the price we pay for open speculation as against conviction. Thus when Browning's Abt Vogler says 'the rest may reason and welcome, 'tis we musicians know', he was saying that the apparent miracle of musical composition (which Browning typically chose to regard metaphysically rather than mathematically) could give man a total insight into divine purpose. But neither through art nor metaphysics could Tennyson achieve such certainty. His mind constantly returned to the limitations of human knowledge: the more we know, as he says in 'The Two Voices', the more obscure is the total design.

Death remains the one barrier to full insight which science cannot overleap.

> Thine anguish will not let thee sleep,
> Nor any train of reason keep:
> Thou canst not think, but thou wilt weep,

So Housman later described man as the being who 'if he thinks, he fastens his hand upon his heart'. And even into Shelley's vision of total freedom sorrow enters because it is an ineradicable part of human nature: 'for oft we still must weep since we are human' is perhaps the most poignant line in the whole of *The Revolt of Islam*. The more we learn, the more elusive truth (as the complete and satisfied assent to the purpose and course of creation) seems.

> . . . in seeking to undo
> One riddle and to find the true,
> I knit a hundred others new.

The 'plain fact' cannot give man assurance: he is the natural sceptic set apart from the rest of creation by his 'dark wisdom', his 'divided will'. (See, again, 'The Higher Pantheism'.) Thus in Tennyson renaissance mind, after three centuries of 'climbing up to knowledge infinite', is seen very near the end of its tether. Even the vision of the summit which has kept him going becomes teasingly obscured:

> Vast images in glimmering dawn,
> Half shown, are broken and withdrawn.

Tennyson is very fond of the word 'half' which for him symbolises the divided will, the divided response. Other key words in 'The Two Voices', many of which recur in *In Memoriam*, are vague, random, dream, dim, dark, veil, hidden, nothing—and a whole series of negatives: not plain, answer not again, nor canst thou show the dead are dead, such as no language may declare, what is it that I may not fear:

> A life of nothings, nothing worth,
> From that first nothing ere his birth
> To that last nothing under earth.

So speaks the barren voice of despair, to which Tennyson is drawn both by temperament and by the grief he feels for Hallam's death. Much of *In Memoriam* is therefore a search for a formula of endurance. Man for Tennyson is a creature who has to keep going despite all the evidence (which is either against him or not proven); and here he draws very close to the humanist position. Not to assume immortality is to make the whole of human history absurd and pointless. Man, despite his inability to find in nature the images of perfection of which his mind— and only his mind—is capable, still cannot stop trying to use life to the utmost:

> 'Tis life whereof our nerves are scant,
> Oh life, not death, for which we pant;
> More life, and fuller, that I want.

Again Tennyson draws close to humanism and again anticipates one of the demands of Shaw and the creative evolutionists.

2. The Phenomenal and the Visionary

Natural descriptions play a large part in Tennyson's work and he is often thought of as our greatest 'nature poet' since Wordsworth. But although both poets emphasised the value of mystical intuition, their attitudes to nature are very different. Wordsworth arrived at a permanent relation with nature, which gave him what Arnold called 'insight into permanent sources of joy and consolation for mankind'. There is no comparable view of nature in Tennyson. After the gloomy colloquy which forms the greater part of 'The Two Voices' the poet wanders out into the woods:

> I wonder'd, while I paced along;
> The woods were fill'd so full of song,
> There seem'd no room for sense of wrong.

He is temporarily cheered up:

> Nature's living motion lent
> The pulse of hope to discontent—

but the sense of wrong obstinately returns, and he records the fact with despondent honesty. One feels he had genuinely hoped for a more positive enlightenment such as Wordsworth had experienced, and is genuinely surprised at his failure to get it:

> I marvell'd how the mind was brought
> To anchor by one gloomy thought.

In *In Memoriam* it is poetic composition, not nature, which brings some consolation after Hallam's death: see XXXVIII:

> No joy the blowing season gives,
> The herald melodies of spring,
> But in the songs I love to sing
> A doubtful gleam of solace lives.

When man despairs, nature cannot comfort him even though (as Tennyson agrees in 'The Higher Pantheism') nature is the manifestation of God:

> Dark is the world to thee: thyself art the reason why,
> For is He not all but that which has power to feel 'I am I'?

> Glory about thee, without thee; and thou fulfillest thy doom,
> Making Him broken gleams, and a stifled splendour and gloom.

The phenomenal world provides no direct link between the mind of God and the mind of man; we take our dark night of the soul with us, even into our contemplation of the natural world. And this is no mere matter of 'fancy' (i.e. delusion) which even Wordsworth sometimes accuses of

> Sending sad shadows after things not sad,
> Peopling the harmless fields with signs of woe:
> Beneath her sway a simple forest cry
> Becomes an echo of man's misery—

but of a fundamental flaw in the human mind.

Tennyson saw nature as the setting for performances and spectacles as intense and as transitory as the emotions which sweep across the mind: sometimes they seem to echo human feelings, but sometimes seem indifferent to them and irrelevant. He was fascinated by these manifestations and recorded them with a novel precision; but they pass, and he passes from them to the sombre and intricate processes of the mind itself. He could be detached about nature; he could look at it without drawing a moral, as when he noticed things like

> the sharp wind that ruffles all day long
> A little bitter pool about a stone
> On the bare coast

or the way a thistle shakes 'when three gray linnets wrangle for the seed'; or in *In Memoriam* LXXII, the way a shower of rain can

> make the rose
> Pull sideways and the daisy close
> Her crimson fringes to the shower;

Like Hardy, Tennyson was 'a man who used to notice such things'. His technique of close observation and accurate description was followed by the Pre-Raphaelites though there is always in their work a touch of studied affectation never found in Tennyson (see, for instance, Rossetti's 'The Woodspurge'). As Professor Willey says, Tennyson had in him 'the ingredients of both landscape painter and field naturalist'.

Tennyson usually saw nature as a collection of separate phenomena: storms, changing light, flowers, etc. (In contrast, Wordsworth characteristically evokes grand static objects which are eternally 'there', like mountains and rocks.) Tennyson also generalised nature: but again, not like Wordsworth as a source of creative insight but rather as an abstract and amoral process. In such aspects nature is for Tennyson classically time-haunted, evoking a mood of sadness rather than joy because emphasising human mortality:

> The woods decay, the woods decay and fall,
> The vapours weep their burthen to the ground,
> Man comes and tills the field and lies beneath,
> And after many a summer dies the swan.

In *In Memoriam*, too, the classical procession of nature underlines human sorrow: see for instance LXXXV:

> But Summer on the steaming floods
> And Spring that swells the narrow brooks,
> And Autumn with a noise of rooks
> That gather in the waning woods,
>
> And every pulse of wind and wave
> Recalls, in change of light or gloom,
> My old affection of the tomb,
> And my prime passion in the grave.

Or the even finer XV:

Tonight the winds begin to rise
   And roar from yonder dropping day:
   The last red leaf is whirl'd away,
The rooks are blown about the skies;

The forest crack'd, the waters curl'd,
   The cattle huddled on the lea,
   And wildly dash'd on tower and tree
The sunbeam strikes along the world.

'Last' emphasises autumnal sadness and the feeling of finality one gets at the onset of winter; rhe rooks being blown suggests the helplessness of creation, at the mercy of chance; 'the world' suggests, what the whole sense at this point of the sequence requires, that when the mind is full of unrest it feels as though every natural phenomenon contributes to this unrest: it wants to involve nature in its own feelings. The characteristic repeated use of the definite article helps towards this feeling of a general state of nature being in tune with the poet's own state of mind.

In the following poem he wonders whether sorrow may not

only seem to take
The touch of change in calm or storm

and goes on to compare himself—in lines which recall some similar line in the very early 'Supposed Confessions of a Second-Rate Sensitive Mind'—to a boat hitting a rock at night: this leads on naturally to the real boat which brought Hallam's body back to England. Thus, at best, nature may perhaps not reflect a man's deepest feelings when he is emotionally lost; but she cannot be expected to stabilise them.

Dark thoughts again correspond to gloomy weather in *In Memoriam* LXXII, the first and more powerful of the two poems on the anniversary of Hallam's death; while in the Wimpole Street poem (VII) the bleak drizzling dawn exactly matches Tennyson's mood of desolation.

Thus Tennyson does not find in nature that source of therapy and spiritual enlightenment of which Wordsworth wrote, e.g. in *Tintern Abbey*:

that blessed mood
In which the burthen of the mystery,
In which the heavy and the weary weight
Of all this unintelligible world
Is lighten'd.

In Tennyson it is the image itself which stands out in isolation, a spectacular moment of emphasis and display. One might almost say that he diminishes the power of nature, not only by subordinating it to human impressions, but by the very richness and precision of his imagery: instead of the austere purifying generalisations which sweep across the pages of Wordsworth, he offers so much technique that we are less conscious of the phenomena themselves, as something we can all experience, than of Tennyson's lavishly differentiated impression of them; and we are reminded of Turner's reply to the complaint that no one else had ever seen sunsets like his: 'Yes, but don't you wish you had.' At its simplest, this technical display is seen in the nature similes in the long poems. Thus the sharp wind that ruffles the stone, quoted above (from *Guinevere*) is compared to a small violence done to Modred which rankles in his heart. But in such similes we are not interested in the other, human side of the comparison. Again, in this fine passage from *The Princess*

> . . . And she as one that climbs a peak to gaze
> O'er land and main, and sees a great black cloud
> Drag inward from the deeps, a wall of night,
> Blot out the slope of sea from verge to shore,
> And suck the blinding splendour from the sand
> And quenching lake by lake and tarn by tarn
> Expunge the world. . . .

we are not interested in the fact that this sight, seen by 'one' (i.e. Tennyson) is compared to the Princess's sadness and solitude: 'so blacken'd all her world', says Tennyson, but clearly this barely stated human black-out cannot match the natural process which sweeps before us in such rich and dramatic detail. The link between man and nature is purely perfunctory. The description is purely decorative; it is self-justifying or it is nothing; it has no structural function.

But in *In Memoriam* the natural descriptions are more complex than this: they do have a structural function. They provide a series of metaphors on the changing state of the poet's mind. A straightforward example is the yew tree in the second poem of the sequence, which sympathises with—indeed seems almost to encourage—the poet's longing for self-surrender; it is as if the tree takes advantage of a temporary weakening of the will.

> And gazing on thee, sullen tree,
>   Sick for thy stubborn hardihood,
>   I seem to fail from out my blood
> And grow incorporate into thee.

'Sick for', i.e. pining for, as in Keats, *Ode to a Nightingale*, vii, 6; but the
sickness of the poet, his failure of will, must also be contrasted with the
gloomy vigour of the tree, here on the point of absorbing the poet in
one of the entranced or self-hypnotised states which result from despair.
In LXXXIII the relation between a prolonged winter and 'the sorrow
in the blood' is more complex and ambiguous.

This animistic treatment of nature, the hint of magical powers, the
emphasis on human feebleness, are paralleled in classical poetry where the
endless cycles of nature are contrasted so often, and so movingly, with
the brief life of man.

> frigora mitescunt zephyris, ver proterit aestas
>   interitura simul
> pomifer autumnus fruges effuderit, et mox
>   bruma recurrit iners.
> damna tamen celeres reparant caelestia lunae:
>   nos ubi decidimus
> quo pater Aeneas, quo dives Tullus et Ancus,
>   pulvis et umbra sumus.

Housman's translation beautifully catches the plangency of Horace's
tamen:

> . . . But oh, whate'er the sky-led seasons mar,
>   Moon upon moon rebuilds it with her beams:
> Come *we* where Tullus and where Ancus are
>   And good Aeneas, we are dust and dreams.

'The violet comes but we are gone'. In the same way nature underlines
the pathos of human mortality in Gray, when he renders the poignancy
of Lucretius's lines beginning 'iam iam non domus accipiet te laeta . . .'
in the *Elegy*: 'For them no more the blazing hearth shall burn . . .'

Tennyson, then, felt in natural phenomena correspondences to his own
moods, but did not seek in nature any underlying associative principle
to which permanent reference could be made. In *In Memoriam* nature
becomes a mechanistic principle, amoral and unfeeling, indifferent to the

claims of man. In this sense Tennyson is speaking of nature in a particularly nineteenth-century way; and we should keep this philosophic
usage separate from the natural descriptions which are in the eighteenth-
century tradition of 'landscape': the striking, composed set-piece done
for dramatic effect. The well-known lines to Virgil then become highly
relevant to Tennyson's own achievement:

> Landscape-lover, lord of language,
>   more than he that sang the Works and Days,
> All the chosen coin of fancy
>   flashing out from many a golden phrase.
>
> Thou that seest universal
>   Nature moved by universal Mind;
> Thou majestic in thy sadness
>   at the doubtful doom of human kind;

Here the distinction is made clear. Nature is the creative principle in
which man's vision tries to find some ground for faith; 'landscape-lover,
lord of language' refers to the artificial arrangement in words of specific
phenomena, the artist's search for the picturesque.

Sometimes in *In Memoriam*, natural descriptions are not only picturesque in their own right but become images, emblems of states of
mind, and thus play an important part in the emotional development of
the poem. Thus in CXV, we begin with a landscape painting of the
ending of winter; and finish with

> and in my breast
> Spring wakens too; and my regret
> Becomes an April violet,
> And buds and blossoms like the rest.

Here Tennyson makes the violet an emblem of his regret because he
feels it has been personal to him long enough: now it becomes part of a
general process which may carry echoes of mortality behind the sense
of reawakening hope, but which at least carries with it the common
experience of all humanity, not just the poet's private burden. The
violet is the common reawakening of spring; 'my' becomes 'an'; it is
as if, already, he cannot say which of all the violets was once his secret
personal regret. His jealously preserved feelings are surrendered to a
shared process of time. Yet the regret is still there, not less valuable for

being no longer identifiable. (So, too, a few poems later, 'every thought breaks out a rose'.) By the irony of time (whose operation is first predicted very early in the sequence) a grief which Tennyson once refused to see in the wider context of all human suffering now takes that place.

Perhaps the most original and striking use of natural objects as emblems of states of mind in all Tennyson's work is to be found in *Maud*, I, xxii ('Come into the garden, Maud'). The power of this lyric derives largely from the contrast between the world of Victorian melodrama (that is, the world of the narrative in which it takes its place) and the intensely private dream-world of the poet-lover. Thus, some of the earlier lines belong to the 'real' world of the narrative: the dance is a real dance, the 'young lord-lover' has kept Maud indoors through the hot summer night until at last the guests leave:

> Low on the sand and loud on the stone
> The last wheel echoes away.

There we are given a precise aural memory. But now the dance music from indoors stops though its rhythm goes on (it is the rhythm of the poem) as the dream music, the garden music, takes over. The strange dialogue which follows has been prepared for while the dance was still going on:

> And the soul of the rose went into my blood
> As the music clash'd in the hall;

and reaches a climax so remarkable that only familiarity can excuse our underestimating it:

> There has fallen a splendid tear
>   From the passion-flower at the gate.
> She is coming, my dove, my dear;
>   She is coming, my life, my fate;
> The red rose cries, 'She is near, she is near',
>   And the white rose weeps, 'She is late';
> The larkspur listens, 'I hear, I hear';
>   And the lily whispers, 'I wait'.

The flowers become the lover and voice his passion. They are not merely witnesses to the drama but participants in it, emblems of his own feelings. The flowers await Maud's coming in a state of violent sexual

anticipation which is transferred to them from the lover. And the start-
ling closing lines, in which the poet says that his dust, if he were dead,
would blossom under Maud's feet 'in purple and red' (colours of blood:
not only the blood of the possessed lover, but the blood to be shed in
the coming duel) suggest not only sexual passion but violence and magic.
Maud can have this effect on the neurotic hero of the poem because she
is in league with nature like the heroine of an E. M. Forster story:
she seems to have taken over the whole countryside as well as the garden
('your rivulet', 'your walks').

Thus strong feelings (passion, despair) can seem temporarily to have
a transfiguring effect on nature, so that the relation between man and
nature can become almost that of conspirators. But the process remains
temporary: it produces the kind of entranced heightening of sensibility
one associates with drugs. The process can be seen again in *In Memoriam*
XCV, the famous nocturnal vision, in which the poet, after noting
how

> the white kine glimmer'd, and the trees
> Laid their dark arms about the field

falls into a trance, surrenders to a transcendental experience in which
Hallam's soul and his own seem to undergo a mystical fusion of the kind
associated with Plotinus and the neoplatonic mystics, a fusion in which
all doubts are resolved (cf. Donne, 'this ecstasie doth unperplex'). But
then, by a characteristic effort of the doubting will (for at this stage he is
still not quite ready to surrender regret) Tennyson recalls himself to
reality:

> At length my trance
> Was cancell'd, stricken thro' with doubt

There, just as they were before the experience, are the white kine and
the dark fields: Tennyson repeats the lines to show that the momentary
'ecstasy' seems to have had no effect on external reality. Yet a change
does ensue: the stillness appropriate to a trance-state is broken, movement begins:

> And suck'd from out the distant gloom
>   A breeze began to tremble o'er
>   The large leaves of the sycamore,
> And fluctuate all the still perfume,

And gathering freshlier overhead,
 Rock'd the full-foliaged elms, and swung
 The heavy-folded rose, and flung
The lilies to and fro, and said

'The dawn, the dawn', and died away;
 And East and West, without a breath,
 Mixt their dim lights, like life and death,
To broaden into boundless day.

These beautiful stanzas form one of the climaxes of the whole sequence and prepare the way for the completer and more specific vision of a few poems later (CIII). Tennyson retains his exact perception of reality (the large leaves of the sycamore) yet the breeze, though a real dawn breeze, also plays an animistic role, participating in, commenting on, the transcendental experience. It speaks like the roses in *Maud*; while in the closing lines the effect of light at dawn is offered both as the description of a phenomenon and as an image of the mixing of life and death into some state of surreality such as occurred during the visionary experience. Once again we see nature in sympathetic assent to a particular human condition; yet if any moral assurance is to be drawn from the experience, it is not nature which supplies it. So this transitory animism corresponds to moments of heightened emotional awareness in the poet. The verse itself emphasises this. The long vowels and monosyllables in

   and right and left
  Suck'd from the dark heart of the long hills roll
  The torrents, dash'd to the vale . . .

or

   when the crimson-rolling eye
  Glares ruin, and the wild birds on the light
  Dash themselves dead

(both from *The Princess*) convey a desire to dramatise the splendour of the particular phenomenon; there is no question of its establishing any general principle.

Thus nature in Tennyson is linked emotively to human experience and comments on it in various ways, but does not open into any new insight or unifying of experience. In *In Memoriam* landscapes play a part which is more Proustian than Wordsworthian, 'mixing memory and desire': memories of Hallam, in Wimpole Street, Cambridge or Somersby. When Tennyson speaks of 'the eternal landscape of the past' he sees human life as a journey: we can keep alive our associations with places we pass through, by memory, or by going back to them, but they will only retain their emotive power over us so long as the association which made them important is cherished: 'and so may Place retain us still'. We see this clearly in *In Memoriam* CI, the famous farewell to Somersby, the 'well beloved place' of Tennyson's childhood. The poet begins by saying that the natural processes so long and lovingly studied by him, details of which he recalls with a wistful exactness, will go on when he has gone, but 'unwatched', 'unloved', 'uncared for':

> Till from the garden and the wild
>   A fresh association blow.
>   And year by year the landscape grow
> Familiar to the stranger's child;
>
> As year by year the labourer tills
>   His wonted glebe, or lops the glades;
>   And year by year our memory fades
> From all the circle of the hills.

And in the next poem, as Tennyson turned to go, the 'pleasant fields and farms', the 'dulcia arva' of Virgil's first eclogue,

>   mix in one another's arms
> To one pure image of regret.

Tennyson here transfers his own strong feeling for place to the place itself: 'our memory' means primarily 'memory of us in the place', and secondarily, our memories of the place which we carry with us in the form of images gradually blending into a vague general memory. Thus places have an 'aura': they belong to those who have known them and loved them, and Tennyson, being a realist, knows that gradually they will come to mean as much to others as they did to him. The eloquence, the moral dignity, of this resignation, look back (like so much in Tennyson) rather than forward: back to the controlled propriety of Marianne's farewell to her family home in Jane Austen's *Sense and Sensibility* (chapter 3):

O happy house! could you know what I suffer in now viewing you
from this spot, from whence perhaps I may view you no more! and
you, ye well known trees! but you will continue the same. No leaf
will decay because we are removed, nor any branch become motion-
less although we can observe you no longer. . . .

In later nature poets this emotional decorum degenerates into a petulant
refusal to surrender proprietary rights; the quality of Tennyson's regret
can be more clearly appreciated if it is compared to, say, Housman's
'Tell me not here' (*Last Poems* XL):

> Possess, as I possessed a season,
>   The countries I resign,
> Where over elmy plains the highway
>   Would mount the hills and shine,
> And full of shade the pillared forest
>   Would murmur and be mine.
>
> For nature, heartless, witless nature,
>   Will neither care nor know
> What stranger's feet may find the meadow
>   And trespass there and go,
> Nor ask amid the dews of morning
>   If they are mine or no.

The first of these two verses is finely controlled; but then Housman
spoils the poem with the petulance of the last verse: he is upset because
nature is not on his side against the rest of mankind. The false pathos of
the verse shows in the language (the weak 'go' adds nothing to the
charge of trespass just made, and the last two lines are absurd: why
should nature ask such a fatuous question? for no reason except that
Housman wants her to be sorry the feet aren't his but still has enough
sense to realise that she won't be). It would be interesting to follow the
growth of a pejorative use of 'nature' in a general sense: in the renaissance the central word for the whole order of creation, the organisation
of man's experience of the phenomenal world; in Wordsworth an
ennobling source of strength and insight; in Tennyson a process indifferent to man which demands a closer compensating scrutiny of the
moral law; in Housman a term almost without meaning.

   Closely as Tennyson observed the processes of nature, they never
achieved a more than temporary harmony with his mind. The storm

passes, the wind drops, the view fades, and the poet is left brooding as
the plaything of natural forces, apparently as helpless as the red leaf
blown by the wind. And the larger, more general laws of geological
change only emphasise the vulnerability of man: so in *In Memoriam*
CXXIII:

> The hills are shadows, and they flow
>   From form to form, and nothing stands;
>   They melt like mist, the solid lands,
> Like clouds they shape themselves and go.
>
> But in my spirit will I dwell
>   And dream my dream and hold it true;
>   For tho' my lips may breathe adieu,
> I cannot think the thing farewell.

However real the phenomenal world seems, science has shown that
through geological aeons even rocks and stones and trees, Wordsworthian symbols of permanence, change. There is no stability, no
finality; and this must be made to chime in with what Tennyson wants
to feel about Hallam's death. The word 'thing', too, has a Wordsworthian ring: the echoing proximity of 'think' helps here—compare
Tintern Abbey 108, 'all thinking things, all objects of all thought'.
Tennyson contrasts scientific truth with spiritual or visionary truth.
Though he accepts the formula which says the dead are gone as irre-
vocably as the lost continents, their final going is not felt to be true.
'The thing' is contrasted with 'my lips' which repeat the formula while
the mind makes the essential reservation: whatever laws there may be
for the universe, there must be other laws for man. Thus the question
asked in LV, 'Are God and Nature then at strife?' is answered. Man's
soul, his visionary power, gives him a special moral relationship with
God. Hence the final, Shelleyan vision of Hallam as triumphant in
nature, eternally 'there':

> Thy voice is on the rolling air;
>   I hear thee where the waters run;
>   Thou standest in the rising sun,
> And in the setting thou art fair.

Although 'mixt with God and Nature', i.e. part of the total process,
Hallam is also the continued object of human love by which he retains
his identity and demonstrates the special role of man in the universe.

There is a poem by Hardy which reaches the opposite conclusion to *In Memoriam* though taking a similar path. In 'He prefers her earthly' Hardy contemplates a sunset and asks the dead woman whom he loved 'And dwell you in that glory-show?' Hardy's answer is that

> You may; for there are strange strange things in being,
>   Stranger than I know.

Hardy admits the possibility because the purposes of creation are not fully understood; and then rejects it, not on intellectual but on emotional grounds: he does not want to believe in a transfiguration, a change of state. He says flatly

> I would not have you thus and there,
>   But still would grieve on, missing you, still feature
>   You as the one you were.

At the beginning of *In Memoriam* Tennyson too would grieve on; but later he wants to stop grieving, or at least to put his grief into a less personal context. So he works through Hardy's attitude, with which he is at first in sympathy, to something more inclusive and less selfish, more in harmony with the possibilities so painstakingly assembled and examined in the poem. Thus his attitude is more mature than Hardy's though at first sight Hardy's might be thought the more noble and more honest: but Hardy's apparent honesty seems to indicate a deliberately arrested emotional state, a lack of that developing response to experience which is so characteristic of *In Memoriam*. What is most striking about Hardy's poem is its bleak static quality, its very preclusion of any possible change of attitude. If this sunset (one feels) can't budge him, nothing will.

As *In Memoriam* proceeds the visionary element in it becomes more important; it provides the only means of getting 'behind the veil' of nature: visionary experience may afford the insight into truth which knowledge fails to give. In *The Princess* Tennyson justifies a prolonged excursion into fantasy by saying that

> maybe wildest dreams
> Are but the needful prelude to the truth

while in *In Memoriam* it is a 'dream of good' which sustains him during his struggle to gain self-control. So in 'The Higher Pantheism' he says

Dreams are true while they last, and do we not live in dreams?

There are three visionary poems in *In Memoriam*: I have already referred to the second of these, XCV. The first is LXIX, 'I dream'd there would be spring no more', with its curious representation of the poet as a Christ figure, a scapegoat, mocked and scorned (earlier in the sequence he had already felt his intense grief would be criticised and misunderstood). The detail of this poem has a dreamlike clarity and vividness: the city streets black with smoke and frost, the people chattering trifles (the public?) and the poet wandering away into the woods like Tolstoi to wear his crown of thorns: the thorns seem dead like winter trees, but are brought to life by an angel who speaks words of comfort. The crown may be grief for the dead man, the obscure words of comfort a dimly-apprehended vision of ultimate good; the idea of resurrection (already introduced into the sequence in the beautiful Lazarus poems XXXI and XXXII) is offered in answer to the scoffers and doubters: 'they' do not realise that in a doomed world some action must be taken. The poet put his sorrow to work on behalf of all men (hence the 'civic crown', the scapegoat's badge worn proudly as a badge of honour). The public do not thank him for airing an intense private grief, but the effort receives divine approval. The poem's difficulties are not helped by its rather odd placing in the sequence: this is an unusually long winter, but two poems later we are commemorating the anniversary of Hallam's death, which occurred in September, so that LXIX might seem better placed between the Christmas poem LXXVIII and the delayed spring poem LXXXIII.

CIII is the vision of Hallam which Tennyson says he had on his last night in Somersby (in 1837, four years after Hallam's death). Here Arthur becomes also King Arthur

> The king who loved me
> And cannot die

and the poet's two heroes are merged into a larger-than-life being whom Tennyson joins on a mystical voyage: the boat they travel in is like Arthur's barge, and one recalls also the eloquent *poésie de départ* of the closing lines of 'Ulysses' and the late lyric 'Crossing the Bar'. The *In Memoriam* poem does not match up to these: the accompanying maidens are uncomfortably Wagnerian and only the sea music, when the more theatrical 'props' of the vision are cast aside, seems to rise towards the height which the poem, by its key position in the sequence, needs to reach:

> Until the forward-creeping tides
>   Began to foam, and we to draw
>   From deep to deep, to where we saw
> A great ship lift her shining sides.

After this poem comes the last Christmas, the last spring, and the 'content' of which this vision of Arthur was the prelude.

Tennyson alludes elsewhere to visionary experiences: in 'The Ancient Sage', for instance, he speaks of escaping from the self and the prison of the phenomenal world into the clarity of Platonic reality, and links this with poetic contemplation—not, as Wordsworth did, with the contemplation of nature:

> For more than once, when I
> Sat all alone, revolving in myself
> The word that is the symbol of myself,
> The mortal limit of the Self was loosed,
> And past into the Nameless, as a cloud
> Melts into Heaven. I touch'd my limbs, the limbs
> Were strange not mine—and yet no shade of doubt,
> But utter clearness, and thro' loss of Self
> The gain of such large life as match'd with ours
> Were Sun to spark—unshadowable in words,
> Themselves but shadows of a shadow-world . . .

Words (like all art, in Plato's view) are two removes from reality, yet only the artist can indicate to a world dedicated to materialism that transcendental values exist and that he has glimpsed them, and that the 'Mount of Vision' is the ultimate goal of human aspiration. Tennyson felt deeply that this visionary world was more 'real' than the phenomenal world of space and time; this is the theme of much of his finest poetry: and of a well-known letter to his wife Emily:

Annihilate within yourself these two dreams of Space and Time. To me the far-off world seems nearer than the present, for in the present is always something unreal and indistinct, but the other seems a good solid planet, rolling round its green hills and paradises to the harmony of more steadfast laws. There steam up from about me mists of weakness or sin, or despondency, and roll between me and the far planet, but it is still there.

3. The Poem

Tennyson at one time thought of calling *In Memoriam* 'Fragments of an Elegy', a title which overstresses the intermittent nature of the poem at the expense of its underlying unity and development. A better pointer is his subtitle 'The Way of the Soul', and his remark, quoted in the *Memoir*, that the poem is a kind of divine comedy beginning with a death and ending with a marriage. The poem moves from the darkness of loss towards the light of hope and future gain: we shall see that both meanings of 'loss', as the opposite of finding and the opposite of gain, are important. Another parallel suggested by the subtitle is with Donne's second anniversary (*The Progresse of the Soule*) which also carries the required domestic note: that is, in Donne's case, a poem primarily intended for the attention and solace of a particular household, and in Tennyson's, a poem primarily intended as an act of autobiography and autotherapy and secondarily as an account of experience which the poet hoped might be of wider service.

The poem, like 'Locksley Hall' and *Maud*, aroused, inevitably, speculation as to the nature and extent of its autobiographical element. One problem was that of chronology. How far does the poem's time-sequence correspond to that of actual events? (One of the chief features of any transmutation of life into art is that the needs of art generally dictate a new tempo.) We know that the poems were not written in the order in which Tennyson, after seventeen years' work, finally arranged them for publication. Three Christmases elapse in the poem but these cannot actually be the first three Christmases after Hallam's death (1833, 1834 and 1835) since the third Christmas is also apparently Tennyson's first after leaving Somersby in 1837.

Another problem (to which Bradley devotes several pages) was Tennyson's supposed borrowings from earlier poets, particularly Herbert (who is echoed several times in the introductory stanzas). A modern reader, familiar with *The Waste Land*, will not find this surprising and will not feel any need to reconcile any such borrowings with the originality of the new poem. More interesting, perhaps, is the way in which Tennyson's reading of Herbert may have taught him something of the technique of dramatising one's difficulties in verse, of conducting spiritual argument. The crude dialogue form of 'The Two Voices' becomes in *In Memoriam* something much more subtle and flexible.

> 'So careful of the type?' but no.
>   From scarped cliff and quarried stone
>   She cries, 'A thousand types are gone:
> I care for nothing, all shall go.'

Nor does it detract from the originality of the poem to suggest that it may to some extent be read as a poet's commonplace book, a *journal intime* in which the entries are separated by time and silence; the working up into a unified whole of material some of which is quite new to English poetry but some of which is so familiar that even in Tennyson's hands its expression hardly rises above the level of the embroidered text:

> Behold, we know not anything;
>   I can but trust that good shall fall
>   At last—far off—at last, to all,
> And every winter change to spring.

In its new context, such a stanza may be enriched by everything else the poet has to say about the future: it is perhaps not too far-fetched to say that the word 'but' in the second line is the most significant word in the stanza, the 'placing' qualificatory key-word by which a commonplace may open into a whole philosophy of experience.

At the other extreme are those sections of the poem in which Tennyson is trying out difficult scientific or metaphysical hypotheses: and here, his anxiety to be accurate and fair, and at the same time to give his own feelings their full weight, produces obscurities of a kind not normally associated with Victorian verse. The once-notorious obscurities of Browning are of a different kind, for Browning will usually be found to be wrapping up quite simple ideas in layers of verbal cotton wool, multiplying examples or analogies and repeating the same idea in different ways, thereby spoiling even his more lyrical poems. In 'Two in the Campagna', this annoying procedure lies open to the reader and even forms the subject of the poem. The thread of a perfectly familiar proposition is compared to a spider's web and the idea is only 'tantalising' because Browning deliberately makes it so; by playing with an idea he reduces its claim on our serious attention.

The difficulties of *In Memoriam* arise, not from elaboration but from compression; not from word-play but from Tennyson's own genuine struggle with difficult ideas and strong emotions. In getting these ideas and emotions under the control of a strict lyric stanza, Tennyson produces a kind of opaqueness—that is, we think we see to the bottom, but find the logic occluded by the very gnomic quality of the utterance. I do not want to imply that Tennyson is cheating—the very reverse is the case. His approach is, *au fond*, tentative and exploratory, but the highly finished form of the stanzas, their technical assurance, seems to imply a corresponding intellectual assurance which Tennyson is far from claiming. He is always in complete control of his imagery, but underneath ideas are being offered and withdrawn, hypotheses are tested and rejected. Tennyson's achievement is that he has left all the evidence of this hard work in the poem without detracting from the poem's authority.

One example of the process I am thinking of is to be seen in Tennyson's use of the word 'and' at the beginning of lines or sentences. I have counted over three hundred instances of this use, in which 'and' carries the emotional force of one of the stronger Greek enclitics, rather than the sequential force of the conjunction; it often introduces a proposition which does not follow logically from its predecessor but which, inevitably, we want to read as if it did. Thus an emotional formula appears disguised as an intellectual argument: it has to do this because no satisfactory argument has been found, because—indeed—the attempt to find such an argument is the subject of the poem. There are some good examples in the introductory stanzas:

(1)　He thinks he was not made to die;
　　　And thou hast made him; thou art just.

(2)　They are but broken lights of thee;
　　　And thou, O Lord, art more than they,

(3)　For knowledge is of things we see;
　　　And yet we trust it comes from thee.

In (1) it does not follow that man is immortal because (like the rest of creation) he is of divine origin and God is just: but emotionally it is central to the poem that this argument should work. Much, therefore, must be understood in that 'and': something like 'for after all, it is thou who hast made man and it would not be fair if thou hadst given him the power to believe himself immortal if in fact he is not'. In (2) the choice of 'and' as the linking word (rather than 'for' or 'since') helps to disguise the vagueness of the emotive line 'they are but broken lights of thee': the lines mean that man is fragmentary, God is wholeness, and a whole must be more than a part. A hypothesis is framed as a gnomic utterance. In (3) 'and yet' conceals some such argument as 'knowledge is of things we see, and our trouble is with the unseen; but God is unseen, and is the source of all knowledge, so why should he not send more knowledge and, ultimately, knowledge of the unseen too?' Tennyson is here offering a favourite speculation: that there is no reason why the causes of man's present despair should not one day be removed.

Such uses of 'and' can be seen as intensified emotive repetitions of a position reached in a previous proposition, carrying with them the force of a new step forward. Moreover, in many lines beginning with 'and' there is a suppressed verb which has to be understood from a previous line: the omission of these verbs contributes to the gnomic and opaque quality of many of the stanzas. Examples are 'and vacant chaff well meant for grain' (VI, 4), 'and those wild eyes that watch the wave' (XXXVI, 15), 'and such refraction of events as often rises ere they rise' (XCII, 16).

Thus the compressed, gnomic quality of so much of *In Memoriam* is often the result of syntactical ellipsis, or apposition, telescoping argument, as in the lines at the end of CVIII:

> 'Tis held that sorrow makes us wise,
> Whatever wisdom sleeps in thee.

'Whatever' suggests that Tennyson does not know what kind of wisdom sleeps in Hallam, though elsewhere in the poem (e.g. in CXIII) there are attempts to define it. The vague generalised adjective combines with the negative verb 'sleeps' to produce a turning away from precision, a gesture towards the hopelessness of defining this important unknown. The two lines must of course be taken with what precedes them, where Tennyson says that all his attempts to scrutinise the mystery of things are 'barren faith' and 'vacant yearnings' and that he'll

> rather take what fruit may be
> Of sorrow under human skies:

but this does not help as much as it seems to. For if the poet would rather learn from his own grief than from Hallam's death ('the second state sublime'), why then should such store be set by Hallam's death? Several thoughts seem to be present at once: (1) a straight eighteenth-century type of antithesis, viz. '*we* can only be made wise by sorrow, but Hallam's wisdom (whatever its nature, and whether or not it be active), is achieved without sorrow'; (2) 'I don't know what kind of wisdom Hallam has, but in any case it is dormant, no use to me'; (3) (connecting up with the return of the same idea in CIX and CXIII) 'if I did not profit by Hallam's wisdom while he lived I cannot expect to do so now he is dead'; and (4) 'if Hallam had lived his wisdom would have helped not only me but the whole age; but now that wisdom is dormant so I can only hope it is true (as they say) that sorrow makes us wise, since this seems to be the only source of wisdom left to me'.

Elsewhere (in LXI) Tennyson does try to pursue Hallam's newly acquired wisdom, but the attempt falters:

> Tho' following with an upward mind
>   The wonders that have come to thee,
>   Thro' all the secular to-be,
> But evermore a life behind.

This suggests that Hallam's wisdom, far from being dormant, still sets the pace for the living. (The word 'secular' is used, as in LXXVI, in its nineteenth-century sense, of the long processes of change, and not in the older sense of 'age-long' given by Bradley—Tennyson would have come across the usage in Lyell's *Principles of Geology* from which an example is quoted in the *N.E.D.*). And the lines in LXXXII

> Eternal process moving on,
>   From state to state the spirit walks

again suggest the dead as active in wisdom and progress. We are told that they achieve insight into the processes of creation not yet fully revealed in time but one day to be revealed; meanwhile the dead can say

> I triumph in conclusive bliss
> And that serene result of all.

But in the first part of *In Memoriam* the partial insight of the living is more real to Tennyson than any speculation about the total insight of the dead. The pessimism of grief can be seen in that curious, baffled 'evermore' in 'evermore a life behind'. Tennyson feels Hallam is always going to have the advantage of his early death, he will always be the one who got there first; he has skipped the years of uncertainty to which Tennyson is condemned. One may dismiss this as simply another example of the humanist fallacy, an inability and a refusal to separate in the mind the two processes of time and eternity; but the confusion is a source of the very real emotional speculations in the first half of the poem, the sense of having been abandoned.

'Whatever' (in the lines just discussed) is one of the large number of negative qualifying words to be found in the early part of *In Memoriam*, where the vocabulary should be compared with that of 'The Two Voices'. They demonstrate the workings of a mind rather than its conclusions:

> I sometimes hold it half a sin
>   To put in words the grief I feel;
>   For words, like Nature, half reveal
> And half conceal the Soul within.

Where a modern poet might admit to a technical difficulty in expressing 'just what I mean'—

> Words strain,
> Crack and sometimes break under the burden

—Tennyson finds a moral and psychological difficulty. He is not even sure that so personal a grief ought to be expressed at all.

We must also distinguish between a genuine doubt as to the propriety of articulation where a profound personal feeling is concerned, and the conventional inarticulateness of the elegist working on commission: Donne for instance:

> Language thou art too narrow, and too weake
> To ease us now: great sorrow cannot speake.

And Tennyson himself, in some lines written to James Spedding on the death of his brother, had said

> Words weaker than your grief would make
> Grief more.

Although *In Memoriam* finishes by being a public poem Tennyson makes it clear that it started as a private one; he says it was begun, not to 'part and prove', not to close 'grave doubts and answers here proposed', but to express, so far as was possible, his own feelings and to find, in the mechanics of versified articulation (which by the mere fact of its *being* versified, necessarily carries with it a suggestion of feelings being arranged, like flowers in a vase) some relief from sorrow. Thus characteristically he anticipates, and deals with as part of the poem itself, any objections that may be raised as to its consistency or its finality. Rather, the poem is a door opening on to a sequence of vistas. It is the poem's therapeutic quality which is first emphasised: it is the end product of compulsive activity:

> But for the unquiet heart and brain
> A use in measured language lies;
> The sad mechanic exercise,
> Like dull narcotics, numbing pain.

(Thus 'I pipe but as the linnet sings' does not mean that the poem is naïve and artless but that he could not help writing it.)

Tennyson further stresses that beneath all our intellectual show we are essentially inarticulate, unable to find words (other than formulas of doubtful value) to express our deepest feelings. And when he speaks in the first part of the poem of trusting 'what I feel is Lord of all' it is the word 'feel' which asks to be stressed; and when he says 'I can but trust that good shall fall', in a stanza already discussed, he at once comments:

> So runs my dream: but what am I?
> An infant crying in the night:
> An infant crying for the light:
> And with no language but a cry.

The 'dream', the ultimate vision of reality, cannot be precisely articulated: the frightened child, like the 'man in wrath' who (in CXXIV) opposes his feelings to materialist theories, is inarticulate because he cannot help it. (And compare 'they called me fool, they called me child', in the crown of thorns poem.) Yet the child's cry and the angry man's claim that his feelings are not to be explained away by science, are both valid responses to experience.

In XIX Tennyson expands the earlier statement (in V) that words

may afford some covering (both protective and definitive) to the naked-
ness of grief; here grief is compared to the tidal movements which
affect the River Wye. As the deeper waters of the Severn flood into the
Wye, the smaller river becomes silent, absorbed in the larger; at the
ebb, the noises of the Wye itself are heard again. This double movement
of waters is finely used to express the imperfect articulation of 'the
deepest grief of all'. The tears that cannot fall are the real tears. As the
poem proceeds, submerged feelings rise towards the surface, they 'rise
in the heart' (see 'Tears, idle tears', in *The Princess*). The whole emphasis
of the early part of the sequence is on the secretness of inner feeling,
while later, this feeling gradually merges (and emerges) into a new view
of experience.

This intense grief with which the poem begins seemed real to Tennyson but he clearly felt others might not find it justifiable. So the prayer
in XIII

> Come, Time, and teach me, many years,
>   I do not suffer in a dream

is precise, and is precisely answered. What times teaches in the poem is
not just that 'loss is common to the race' (a lesson which Tennyson
rejects early in the sequence as irrelevant) but that it is a part of experience which, though it seemed to exist as a dream in a brain disordered
by grief, is in fact something each man must master, assimilate and
accept as part of the total pattern of human experience. Thus the poem
is addressed both to the reader who comes to doubt but stays to understand, and to the poet himself, and one can see passages in which the
one or the other audience is uppermost in the poet's mind. The poem's
popularity shows that the Victorians felt Tennyson had not only done
something for himself, turned loss into gain, which would have appealed
to their practical sense, but had also done something for humanity at
large. Individual experiences of loss are not weakened by repetition but
intensified. The clamour of the indifferent, the false attempts to use
scientific theory to discredit human hopes, only emphasise the importance of Tennyson's undertaking. And the final dismissal of theory by
personal feeling in

> And like a man in wrath the heart
>   Stood up and answer'd 'I have felt',

is significant because it is not *my* heart but the heart of man; so, too, in the closing poems of the cycle Tennyson changes from 'I' (I shall not lose thee tho' I die) to 'we': the pooling of experience increases the stature of man.

The poem has three time values. There is the present—grief and suffering—to which we must add that the poem's present is itself offered to the reader as a grief past and overcome. This is emphasised by the introductory stanzas, written in 1849, the year before the poem was published and sixteen years after it was begun: so that the words

> Forgive my grief for one remov'd . . .
> Forgive these wild and wandering cries

are among the first we read. Though addressed to 'the strong Son of God, immortal Love' they seem equally to be addressed to the reader, a characteristic attempt to forestall criticism.

The second time value is the past: memories of Hallam, arousing the nostalgia with which the poem is commonly associated ('thinking of the days that are no more'). There is finally the future: speculation as to Hallam's new state, the relation between the living and the dead, and a possible connection between man's gradual evolution on earth as a race and his instant evolution in heaven as an individual (see CXVIII discussed in Chapter 1).

The present is the felt and recorded desire to surrender to despair and the moral struggle not to (see for instance IV in which darkness and sleep, a 'type' of death, temporarily conquer the will). The past is places where Tennyson and Hallam were together, e.g. the Cambridge poem LXXXVII. The future is opaque, the battleground of faith and doubt, the realm of speculation which at first seems useless because irresoluble and is only gradually worked out into an acceptable pattern. It is here that Tennyson has to work hardest to reconcile personal feelings with, intellectual hypothesis. He feels it to be the poet's duty to do this, to set his personal feelings into the context of the whole of human experience, however distasteful (at first) or difficult the process seems. Thus, in XXXIV, he says that if there were no immortality the poet could set aside moral considerations and concentrate on aesthetic ones. The need to believe in a moral purpose in man's creation requires a corresponding sense of moral purpose in the poet. Death, and the grief it brings to the living, is at first noted as an intolerable evil, a black mark against the universe. In LV death is seen as part of the natural process and the wish to believe man an exception, an 'evil dream'. The poem's triumph is that it converts this evil dream into a dream of good, and finally into the total reality of man's experience.

> O yet we trust that somehow good
> Shall be the final goal of ill

'O yet', that is, despite evidence to the contrary; 'somehow', that is, in ways of which science is still ignorant. Yet the imperative 'shall' observes that any other conclusion is intolerable, and points away from the tentative half-hearted faith of the opening poems (expressed in words like 'failing', 'faltering', 'grope', etc.) towards the triply repeated formula of acceptance, 'all is well', with which the poem ends and which recalls the words of Dame Julian of Norwich quoted at the end of T. S. Eliot's *Four Quartets*: 'and all shall be well'.

Thus *In Memoriam* is a journey from doubt and despair to acceptance, a journey through time and experience, in which past, present and future co-exist, and in which different modes of experience (memory, speculation, vision) all find a place. As T. S. Eliot says in *Burnt Norton* 'only through time time is conquered'; and again in *The Dry Salvages*:

> Here the impossible union
> Or spheres of existence is actual
> Here the past and future
> Are conquered and reconciled

At the start of the poem Tennyson wants to remain fixed in grief, in the total absorption of loss; he resists the processes of time by which grief may (and as time itself will show, must) be conquered. But he is not immediately prepared to

> reach a hand thro' time to catch
> The far-off interest of tears.

The idea of loss is central to the poem: financial imagery occurs in several places, e.g. gain, credit, influence-rich all occur in LXXX. Here, present loss may be eventual profit but Tennyson does not yet want to be comforted by borrowing on the doubtful security of this future dividend. Grief is his only immediate asset and he is not yet ready to risk it on a theory he has not yet tested. He repulses the 'victor hours' (the effects of time) and in the yew tree poem (II) seems ready to identify himself with the tree, as a symbol of unchanging gloom. One notices the word 'fail' at this point: the sense is that of the poet's life-processes running down in sympathy with Hallam's: there is a strong desire to 'cease'. So too in L, the prayer of the sinking soul, in which Tennyson anticipates his own death. In this poem, again, there is the feeling (helped by the monosyllables) of time being halted, natural processes being slowed down almost to a stop:

> Be near me when my light is low,
>   When the blood creeps and the nerves prick
>   And tingle; and the heart is sick,
> And all the wheels of Being slow . . .

This mood persists even after the return of Hallam's body to England and the burial. In XXVI, however, time begins to show its strength and the poet must struggle to keep his grief perpetually present. Can love survive time and separation? The desire (and the need) to prove that it can begins: the victor hours are already showing their hand:

> Still onward winds the dreary way;
>   I with it; for I long to prove
>   No lapse of moons can canker Love,
> Whatever fickle tongues may say.

In the early part of the sequence love is still identified with grief, grief seen as the only true evidence of enduring love: 'let love clasp grief lest both be drowned' in the victor hours poem precisely formulates the poet's early need: he 'still would grieve on'. But already in that characteristic 'I long to prove' the first doubt as to time's power to change one's feelings is, half apprehensively, admitted. Later in the same poem (XXVI) he says that if love does turn to indifference and there is no immortality, then he would despise his grief and wish for death. This idea is taken up again in XXXV, a subtler version of 'The Two Voices'. The argument here is (1) even if all things die, it is still worth loving for love's own sake:

> Might I not say? 'Yet even here,
>   But for one hour, O Love, I strive
>   To keep so sweet a thing alive:'

But (2) the objection to this comes from love itself; the very nature of love would be altered if there were no immortality: love would be 'half dead to know that it would die'. And (3) the nineteenth-century evolutionists put in their warning:

> But I should turn mine ears and hear
>
> The moanings of the homeless sea,
>   The sound of streams that swift or slow
>   Draw down Aeonian hills and sow
> The dust of continents to be;

The known, reachable, comfortable limits of human life are contrasted with the formless and homeless sea, outside the control of *homo domesticus*. (One thinks of 'the unplumb'd salt estranging sea' in Arnold's 'Marguerite' and the desolation of his 'Dover Beach'.) The processes of creation seem to be on the wrong side. But (4) the poet rejects the fruitless hypothesis:

> If Death were seen
>   At first as Death, Love had not been,
> Or been in narrowest working shut . . .

Tennyson here adduces his own experience of love as evidence for immortality. While paying lip-service to scientific formulas, he insists that man may be an exception to whatever rules these seem to prove. Otherwise, human love could never have been experienced. Here we must bear in mind Tennyson's deep sense of waste: so much love concentrated into so few years must somehow be made to go on being valuable; in the same way, the whole splendour of human achievement through history becomes pointless if man is a doomed race (see LVI). Throughout the poem Tennyson links the immortality of the individual with that of the race. Like the seventeenth-century elegists, he has to come to terms with a divine law which can cut good men off in their prime: will the same law, one day, cut off the whole race? The seventeenth century could draw a theological moral from premature death and even, with a little ingenuity, find in it a positive gain; but Tennyson, far more involved in Hallam than was Jonson in Salomon Pavy or Donne in Lord Harrington, finds it harder to take refuge in neat and pious formulas. Of course *In Memoriam* is not really about Hallam at all, but about Tennyson after Hallam's death. Thus it is his own intense feelings that at first prevent him from seeing Hallam's death (as Donne saw Harrington's) as some kind of triumphant achievement on Hallam's part. The triumph, when it comes, is Tennyson's rather than Hallam's. Donne used the elegy, as the patron would have required him to do, to praise the dead man; Tennyson specifically refuses to use *In Memoriam* to praise Hallam (see LXXV), partly because his achievement was less than his potential (a seventeenth-century elegist would have been expected to use all his literary skill to get round this, but Tennyson knew that the Victorian world

> which credits what is done
> Is cold to all that might have been);

and partly because he is unable to convey Hallam's qualities to those who did not know him (see XII). People must deduce those qualities from the strength of the poet's grief and love. It is not until near the end of the sequence, in the rather uninteresting poems CIX-CXI, that any attempt is made to describe Hallam. We then learn that he was a good critic, logical, moral, not ascetic, freedom-loving, beautiful, a good influence on others, and a gentleman. But the picture that emerges is too idealised, and comes too late in the poem, to be significant.

Tennyson makes it clear that while Hallam lived no thought of time's destroying their friendship entered his mind. In LXXXIV he supposes that, if Hallam had lived to old age and they had both died at roughly the same time, there would have been no problem: Christ would have taken them 'as a single soul'. But now the link is broken:

> But thou art turn'd to something strange,
> And I have lost the links that bound
> Thy changes;

The words used here (in XLI) imply, as they must be intended to, the interruption of a happy and well-tried domestic routine which can never be resumed. In the longest poem in the sequence (LXXXV), in which Tennyson, with characteristic honesty and conscientiousness, excuses himself for again thinking of other, earthly friendships, the point is stressed that, however Hallam's new state is to be conjectured, nevertheless

> in dear words of human speech
> We two communicate no more.

From the grief of the living left behind Tennyson turns, in XLIV and some later poems, to the conjectured state of the dead. Perhaps after all the link may not be quite broken: the dead may retain images of their former life as well as their new knowledge. Tennyson suggests that these intimations of mortality may be comparable to the intimations received by the living either of a previous existence (but this primitive idea of reincarnation, though found in 'The Two Voices', is dropped in *In Memoriam*) or of the earliest, forgotten days of life. During our first year after birth we have no conscious processes; then we begin to be self-conscious. Individualisation is a mental process. This is most interestingly stated in XLV:

> The baby new to earth and sky,
>   What time his tender palm is prest
>   Against the circle of the breast,
> Has never thought that 'this is I'.
>
> But as he grows he gathers much,
>   And learns the use of 'I' and 'me',
>   And finds 'I am not what I see,
> And other than the things I touch'.
>
> So rounds he to a separate mind
>   From whence clear memory may begin,
>   As thro' the frame that binds him in
> His isolation grows defined.

In these fine lines the word 'isolation' carries undertones of a sadness not strictly required, since its primary meaning here is purely technical (bio-physical). But Tennyson is also thinking of another kind of isolation. Love is the coming together of two isolates: thought-processes can only operate through language. In the last verse of this poem Tennyson draws a speculative conclusion:

> This use may lie in blood and breath,
>   Which else were fruitless of their due,
>   Had man to learn himself anew
> Beyond the second birth of Death.

This ties up with the feeling of waste which prompted the argument for immortality deduced from the preciousness of love; but the lines have a further implication: that if we never grew up on earth we should have to go through the process in heaven. Death must be an advance on life, not a mere repetition of it. Self-knowledge must be carried over and incorporated into the new knowledge, the 'conclusive bliss' and insight into 'that serene result of all' offered by death. But the use of 'may' suggests that Tennyson is not entirely happy about his hypothesis, though Shaw would not have found it absurd. Life involves considerable effort, and Tennyson does not want to feel that this effort is wasted: but it would not be wasted if (1) there were a 'second birth of death'; and (2) man carried over into this the habits formed in life. Man would be in a better position to concentrate on the new knowledge made available after death if he did not at the same time have to try to re-establish his own identity. In the preface to his evolutionary play *Back to Methuselah*, in which he seeks to replace Darwinism with the earlier theories of Lamarck (who believed that the life force, the will, not the blind force of natural selection, was the cause of evolution) Shaw writes 'the moment we form a habit we want to get rid of the consciousness of it so as to economise our consciousness for fresh conquests of life'. Like Shaw, Tennyson is constantly trying to put back into evolutionary theory the spiritual element which Darwinism, it seemed, was about to discard; like Shaw, too, he felt that the greatest stumbling-block to man's moral progress was the shortness of his life and the inevitability of his death. Only by getting over this obstacle could he see a way out of the mechanistic heresy; and he got over it by positing death as a develop-ment in the individual paralleling the development of the race on earth, rather as the embryo's nine months in the womb takes it through ages of natural selection from primitive cell to highly developed organism, yet still leaves it only at the beginning. So in 'The Ancient Sage' he speculates:

> Who knows? or whether this earth-narrow life
> Be yet but yolk, and forming in the shell?

Like Shaw, Tennyson felt that human life must somehow be prolonged if it is not to be cruel and pointless, and this would have seemed par-ticularly important when a man died young as Hallam did; he needed to feel that its unused potential ('the force that would have forged a name') was retained for some new activity:

> I know transplanted human worth
> Will bloom to profit otherwhere;

and again, in LXXV, he is thinking of the waste which, without an evolutionary immortality, Hallam's death must have been:

> But somewhere, out of human view,
> What'er thy hands are set to do
> Is wrought with tumult of acclaim.

Tennyson cannot relinquish the idea of Gray's 'applause of list'ning senates to command', the

> Hands, that the rod of empire might have sway'd
> Or wak'd to ecstasy the living lyre.

Although Gray's dead missed high achievement by leading a quiet life not a short one, Hallam does become a village Hampden, a Cromwell guiltless of his country's blood; this is clear from LXIV, from which I quoted at the beginning of Chapter 1. In that poem Hallam, looking back from eternity upon his life on earth, is compared to a man of humble origins who has risen to high place while Tennyson, left behind on earth, becomes the boyhood friend who

> in the furrow musing stands:
> 'Does my old friend remember me?'

And in LX and XCVII Tennyson again casts himself in an inferior role and looks up to Hallam. All these poems emphasise the way in which Tennyson tries to think of Hallam's death as a success story, a kind of promotion. By advancing in heaven and not on earth Hallam finds achievement without its concomitant disappointments and misunder-standings. Like Adonais

> From the contagion of the world's slow stain
> He is secure.

But besides positing for Hallam the triumphs he missed on earth, Tennyson wants him also to remember the happy life they shared on earth, memories of which he himself still retains. Again, this is part of the feeling that nothing must be lost, that there must be continuity; what seems to have been lost must be seen as gain. Time lost is time wasted and the poem is a protest against that proposition. The link which seemed in the first time of grief to have been broken is replaced by 'some strong bond which is to be'.

I have said that it is wrong to think of Tennyson as a crude meliorist. He accepts the evidence of the evolutionists, but transferred to human history this requires (as scientists themselves saw) modification. The roar

E

of traffic is not necessarily an improvement on the stillness of the central sea, but man must evolve to ever nobler ends since any other kind of change would be a counsel of despair. This cannot be proved, though man's previous record may be an argument in its favour, and attempts to prove it are gradually abandoned in favour of gestures towards the 'larger hope' and other vague and distant ends 'to which the whole creation moves'. Knowledge being concerned only with the phenomenal cannot help here, but wisdom can; and by this, as we have seen, Tennyson meant insight into moral law gained through experience, or, as he said in 'Oenone', 'self-reverence, self-knowledge, self-control' (the last term recurs in the last stanza of *In Memoriam*). Thus we learn a kind of stretching out of human dignity beyond the present limits of science and what T. S. Eliot called 'the lifetime of one man only'.

The importance of love, which has directed the whole poem, is that it can make such leaps into the dark seem both intelligible and valuable. So the introductory stanzas are addressed to the 'Strong Son of God, immortal Love'. When Tennyson personifies God it is usually as Christ and usually periphrastically, as 'He that died in Holy Land' (compare *Lycidas*, 'Him who walked the waves').

Moreover, love is not a vague emotion but a powerful specific. In CXXVIII, Tennyson says that his love for Hallam is related to, but is greater than, faith in man's moral evolution—the second pillar upon which the poem's structure is built. He argues that if time is a mere process of change and decay it would offer man no hope: the so-called evolutionary process, instead of being a progress to ever nobler ends, would merely be the blind mutations of chance. Love, having been tested by experience, is stronger than faith in the related, but unverifiable, concept of spiritual evolution. Tennyson's love for Hallam has defied time and death: it is

> The love that rose on stronger wings,
> Unpalsied when he met with Death

And the line, stated twice in CXXVI, 'Love is and was my Lord and King', underlines the central significance of love, both as personal experience tested through time, and as a principle operating in the universe through Christ. What is to be admired in the poem is the way it reconciles a traditional renaissance individualism with the contemporary emphasis on the species: the close view and the long view.

Thus *In Memoriam* is itself an example of the process of moral evolution which it describes. Its value as a record of experience on the two levels of personal suffering and intellectual speculation, lies in the fact that it demonstrates how man can progress from despair both about the 'type' and about the 'single life' to a position in which both may be secured against destruction. In CXVII, another poem addressed to conquered time—the 'days and hours' which had at the beginning of the cycle seemed enemies of love—Tennyson again stresses his acceptance of his role in time. His ultimate meeting with Hallam, of which he is by now sure, will be 'fuller gain' (after the repeated use of the word 'loss' at the beginning of the cycle the use of 'gain' is significant)

> For every grain of sand that runs,
>   And every span of shade that steals,
>   And every kiss of toothed wheels
> And all the courses of the suns.

The stanza emphasises the poet's time-consciousness. He knows now that life has to be lived through moment by moment and that, until his life's end, he will be subject to the processes of time. But his 'proper place' is with Hallam: he reverts to the feeling of a broken link which must be renewed if his love is to have any meaning. He is prepared to be isolated from Hallam through time, but only because he believes that his love will be resumed beyond time.

Thus Tennyson reconciles two attitudes to the dead Hallam: his feeling, while he himself is still alive, that Hallam's presence can be felt by him as part of the universe; and his belief that, after his own death, 'I shall know him when we meet'. Hallam's metamorphosis, then, is itself subordinate to Tennyson's timebound state; it exists only in his mind as a means of turning grief into acceptance. When Tennyson himself quits time, he will no longer need to imagine Hallam as 'standing in the rising sun'. Thus (as is stated in CXXIX) Hallam is at once far off and near; part of a 'dream of good' and an immortal recognisable being waiting for Tennyson to follow him out of time. This I take to be the significance of the words

> Strange friend, past, present and to be;
>   Loved deeplier, darklier understood.

Hallam is 'strange' because he now has a double existence: as part of

Tennyson's timebound philosophy and as an eternal being existing outside time. Again, T. S. Eliot in the *Four Quartets* comes nearest of any later poet to expressing the complex idea resolved in *In Memoriam*, when he says

> See, now they vanish,
> The faces and places, with the self which, as it could, loved them,
> To become renewed, transfigured, in another pattern.

4. *The Epilogue*

I have tried to show that if *In Memoriam* is read as Tennyson intended it to be, the poems of grief and despair at the beginning of the cycle cannot be extracted from the sequence and given special emphasis as though they were representative of the whole poem. The Victorians did not make this mistake, but some modern critics have tended to see in the poem a reflection of our modern static mental condition, even though this means ignoring, or at best belittling, the considerable intellectual and spiritual hard work done in the later poems of the cycle. The cynic of today may smile at the thought that Queen Victoria found in *In Memoriam*, next to the Bible, her best comfort after Albert's death; yet it is hard to see how, if the Queen had read the poem as, say, Mr. T. S. Eliot seems to have read it, she could have found much comfort in it. The slick answer here is, of course, that the Victorians found what *they* wanted and we find what *we* want; that we are more impressed by the documentation of despair than by the documentation of hope; and that, anyway, what Tennyson thought he had achieved may not correspond to what he did achieve. But Tennyson was a highly conscious and self-conscious artist, and a man of the highest intelligence and sensibility. Seventeen years after Hallam's death, he would not have taken the trouble to arrange the poem as he did, and to work out the concluding arguments of the sequence, if he had wanted to leave the poem as a poem of despair (even if it was, in Mr. Eliot's words, despair of a religious kind).

The early poems of the sequence, like VII ('Dark house by which once more I stand') linger in the reader's mind because they speak to our condition, they can be fitted into the tradition of urban *angoisse* established by Baudelaire, Verlaine and Rimbaud; Tennyson's London is the London, it seems, of *The Waste Land*, 'flaring like a dreary dawn'. For the modern reader, using the two-column collected edition of Tennyson, *In Memoriam* is stuffed like a collection of miscellanea into the middle of a cabin trunk, with the result that the sequence seems a mere collection of lyrics, inviting us to pick and choose. In the poem as originally published, in an octavo volume of over two hundred pages, each poem starting on a fresh page, it is somehow much easier to trace a development (as in Meredith's sequence *Modern Love*). Moreover, it must not be forgotten that the great English elegies, *Lycidas* or *Adonais*, always move from personal grief towards the acceptance of some kind of immortality (whether orthodox Christian or pantheistic) which triumphs over grief. Consequently, to give the earlier grief-dominated poems too much emphasis is to place too much strain on a part of the whole, to alter the poem's structure, to reduce its stature, to ignore Tennyson's own intentions and the tradition in which he is writing.

That the poem moves away from despair is particularly (some critics would say over-) emphasised in the epilogue, which celebrates the marriage of Tennyson's sister Cecilia with Edmund Lushington. This marriage took place in 1842, eight years before the publication of *In Memoriam*, so that it cannot be seen as a last-minute addition, tagged on in order to provide a happier happy ending. Indeed, it is clear from the poem's opening stanzas that the epilogue was composed as an epithalamium on and for the occasion itself, so that its incorporation into *In Memoriam* as the poet's last word must have been deliberate.

In the epilogue Tennyson looks back on his own grief, already at the time of writing eight years away and by the time of publication seventeen years. He contrasts his old mood with his present one, which he describes, rather loftily, as

> No longer caring to embalm
> In dying songs a dead regret,
> But like a statue solid-set,
> And moulded in colossal calm.

This is reasonable if one takes Tennyson to mean (what the closing poems of the sequence have already announced) that he has exorcised his grief, subsumed it in a new understanding and acceptance: all passion spent. But the image seems to do rather more than this: the words 'embalm', 'dead' and 'statue' suggest that all feeling has gone, that the poet is no longer capable of feeling and does not wish to be. 'Colossal' is of course directly suggested by 'statue' (the Colossus of Rhodes) but in its ordinary modern sense the adjective nevertheless makes a heavy claim, as if of some larger-than-life stability. After the humility, the self-effacement, the subordination of the self to Hallam's memory, made in the poem, the epilogue seems to show Tennyson as self-aggrandising, boasting about the impressiveness of his new state. He does, it is true, also say that though regret is dead, love is more, but to this he adds that in the last few years

> I myself with these have grown
> To something greater than before.

In the poem itself it was Hallam, and Tennyson's love, that grew vaster and finally became all-pervasive. Now Tennyson appears to be making this claim for himself. Consequently, critics have tended to dismiss the epilogue (even Bradley said the style of its writing was mannered) and have used it to support their argument that the more hopeful note of the later poems is a false one.

I think Tennyson took the marriage as an omen, the symbol of a new start. He may have felt in its finality a residue of discomfort and disloyalty to Hallam for which he had to compensate by citing his own changed attitude. But the attitude has been completely prepared for: it is the self-control achieved at the end of the cycle. The forward-looking tone of the epithalamium is prepared for as early as LXXXV, in which Tennyson admits that he is beginning to be more interested in the future than in the past and feels the need to apologise to Hallam for appearing to desert him, the work of autotherapy and commemoration being already almost complete. The two statements that he counts it 'crime to mourn for any overmuch' and that he cannot forget 'the mighty hopes that make us men' are a warning that the point of no return between past and future is about to be reached.

Tennyson does not expect others to learn wisdom from his experiences if he cannot learn any himself; the epilogue is evidence that he had learnt something, and that what he has learnt is not only self-control but *self-confidence*. In the hour of despair man feels small in his helplessness, and when things go well with him again he seems to fill out, to assert himself again, to take up room on earth proudly instead of trying to creep into a corner and disappear. Moreover, self-control means, not that one has ceased to feel but that one does not *appear* to feel. One is no longer vulnerable. (Tennyson does not say that he *is* a statue but that he is *like* one.) The calm of the epilogue recalls the calm despair of XI: but that calm was as uncontrollable as a calm before a storm, ready at any moment to give way to another onrush of wild unrest. In contrast, the new calm is impervious to external influence (nature's moods are as irrelevant now as they seemed relevant then). So the lines may be taken quite literally: regret *is* dead; we recall

> . . . and my regret
> Becomes an April violet . . .

The violet goes, but we remain: no longer the slaves of our feelings or of our mortality. And the statue is a work of art, and it is through a work of art that Tennyson has achieved his new strength and insight.

But the most important part of the epilogue is the last six stanzas, for they state, more firmly than anything in the preceding poem, Tennyson's faith in the moral evolution of man. Here he re-affirms his belief that a race will one day be born which shall 'look on knowledge'. Of this race Hallam is called a 'noble type, appearing ere the times were ripe'. The idea here is one of correspondence, a familiar one in Christian art: Hallam is to the race to be what an Old Testament figure was to a New Testament one: a prophetic emblem. (But throughout his work Tennyson uses 'type' both in its old theological sense and in its nineteenth-century scientific sense, of a group of organisms having a common pattern. If a perfect specimen of any group can be found, this will serve as a model, exemplar or ideal. The whole article on 'type' in the N.E.D. should be read.) Tennyson thus reinforces as a belief amounting to a prediction what in CXVIII had been a hope, a prayer: 'let the ape and tiger die'. The marriage by turning the poet's mind towards the future gives him new encouragement to believe that man will improve and be 'no longer half akin to brute'. The children of the marriage will be one step nearer the generation which will justify the whole troublesome human experiment: they will be

> a closer link
> Betwixt us and the crowning race

Tennyson is careful not to say when this will be, and CXXVII, one of the few political poems in the sequence, shows that he felt further troubles and upheavals would have to be endured but that the enlightened dead could look beyond these revolutions and smile, knowing what was to follow.

Thus *In Memoriam* ends with the assertion of a regenerative principle as do the last plays of Shakespeare: but a regenerative principle for which we may have to wait patiently through many generations. Meanwhile, man's development on earth is, as we have seen in previous evolutionary poems in the sequence, paralleled by the instant development of the good man in heaven. So Hallam both foreshadows the crowning race and catches up with it in heaven; the dead and the unborn share an insight for which the living seek in vain. And the 'one far-off divine event to which the whole creation moves' is the arrival of the regenerative principle itself, when the long heartbreaking process will be complete. A late poem called 'The Making of Man' makes this clear (again the tiger and the ape represent stages left behind in the process of spiritual evolution):

> Where is one that, born of woman, altogether can escape
> From the lower world within him, moods of tiger or of ape?
> Man as yet is being made, and ere the crowning Age of ages,
> Shall not aeon after aeon pass and touch him into shape?
>
> All about him shadow still, but, while the races flower and fade,
> Prophet-eyes may catch a glory slowly gaining on the shade,
> Till the people all are one and all their voices blend in choric
> Hallelujah to the Maker 'It is finish'd. Man is made.'

We should remember that the idea of a better race was current in the nineteenth century. Mill wrote that Bentham 'lived in a generation of the leanest and barrenest men whom England had yet produced, and he was an old man when a better race came in with the present century'. In the *Idylls* Arthur's knights are called 'the fair beginners of a nobler time'; and Wordsworth in *The Excursion* prayed that his life should 'express the image of a better time' and asked why the vision of Paradise should be

> A history only of departed things
> Or a mere fiction of what never was.

Thus I do not feel with Mr. Eliot that the faith of *In Memoriam* is a poor thing but that it follows a great tradition of faith in what Wordsworth called 'sovereign man'; nor do I feel that the poems of Hardy and Housman (to which I have referred already in this essay) or Thomson's *City of Dreadful Night* with its bleak, mannered pessimisms are characteristic derivatives. What all these writers lack, and what Tennyson and Wordsworth possessed and show in all their work, is piety. This does not preclude feelings of despondency and despair: but it does involve a faith in the existence of something larger, both in human capacity and in the universe as man reads it: and this the late romantic pessimists—egotists whose egotism remained their goal instead of being their philosophic springboard—conspicuously lacked. If I had to single out a poem which obviously derives from *In Memoriam*, I should pick J. A. Symonds's 'A Vista':

> These things shall be! A loftier race
> Than e'er the world hath known, shall rise
> With flame of freedom in their souls
> And light of knowledge in their eyes.

The concept of the golden age is one of the oldest in European poetry, but for Tennyson it is the ultimate goal, never yet attained, an improvement on, not a repetition of, prelapsarian perfection.

What Tennyson claims in *In Memoriam* is that he has won a significant spiritual victory not only over personal despair—

> not in vain,
> Like Paul with beasts, I fought with Death

—but over the false general pessimism engendered by scientific materialism, the dead end of up-to-dateness:

> I think we are not wholly brain,
> Magnetic mockeries . . .

> Not only cunning casts in clay:
> Let Science prove we are, and then
> What matters Science unto men,
> At least to me? I would not stay.

And this argument came to be accepted by Victorian scientists. In his book on *Darwinism*, which appeared in 1889 and which ends with a quotation from *In Memoriam*, A. R. Wallace, arguing that the process of natural selection cannot account for man's spiritual qualities, wrote:

> We who accept the existence of a spiritual world can look upon the
> universe as a grand consistent whole adapted in all its parts to the
> development of spiritual beings capable of indefinite life and per-
> fectibility. To us the whole purpose, the only *raison d'être* of the world
> —with all its complexities of physical structure, with its grand
> geological progress, the slow evolution of the vegetable and animal
> kingdoms, and the ultimate appearance of man—was the development
> of the human spirit in association with the human body.

Thus the vision with which *In Memoriam* ends may be read as a new
metaphor for man's innate capacity for moral greatness, a capacity to
which all the major poets of the eighteenth and early nineteenth centuries
had borne witness. Tennyson thus stands almost at the end of a tradition:
'And the great Aeon sinks in blood'. The value of *In Memoriam* lies in
the fact that in it not only Tennyson's spiritual survival but man's is at
stake. He moves on from despair with a Bunyanesque steadfastness
which we ought to admire in him as he admired it in Hallam:

> He faced the spectres of the mind
> And laid them.

Three years before, in *The Princess*, Tennyson had published some
lines which closely correspond to the end of *In Memoriam*, lines cele-
brating marriage as the symbol of hope not only for the two concerned
but for the human race:

> And so these twain, upon the skirts of Time,
> Sit side by side, full-summ'd in all their powers,
> Dispensing harvest, sowing the To-be,
> Self-reverent each and reverencing each;
> Distinct in individualities,
> But like each other ev'n as those who love.
> Then comes the statelier Eden back to men:
> Then reign the world's great bridals, chaste and calm:
> Then springs the crowning race of human kind.
> May such things be!

To this the practical princess says 'I fear they will not': the poet-prince
replies 'Dear, but let us type them now'. Hallam 'typed' (i.e. both pre-
figured and perfectly exemplified) what man can become: a married
couple can do more, they can take a practical step towards the crown-

ing race. One recalls, reading these lines, Adam and Eve, the slow climb back to Paradise: yet not the old Paradise of innocence, but a new and better Paradise to which accumulated experience and moral wisdom contribute. Meanwhile, the individual can only do his best within existing limitations:

> O we will walk this world,
> Yok'd in all exercise of noble end,
> And so thro' those dark gates across the wild
> That no man knows.

The journey may be long, but man must go on, keeping the vision in his mind; he dies, and all his generation die, but his successors take up the pursuit.

> And we, the poor earth's dying race, and yet
> No phantoms, watching from a phantom shore
> Await the last and largest sense to make
> The phantom walls of this illusion fade,
> And show us that the world is wholly fair,

These lines from 'The Ancient Sage' are perhaps the finest summing up of the Tennysonian vision. Phantom is a favourite word of Tennyson's, and 'phantom shore' also occurs in the poem to Virgil. But man is no phantom, because human vision, and only human vision, can see beyond the phenomenal world. The crowning race will be endowed with the 'last and largest sense' which will allow it to see reality, not through a glass darkly, but clearly. The 'dream of good' from which man now keeps waking because of the limitations of his own mental darkness, is an inkling of that perfection 'behind the veil'.

Man's capacity to understand his limitations, to grasp his predicament, and to place it in a larger context of human development, began to decline during the last decades of the nineteenth century. The visionary power and the steadfastness began to fade. One sees this clearly in Arnold, prophet of modern *angst*. Lines like

> Still the same ocean round us raves
> But we stand still and watch the waves

express the static nature of modern impotence, and emphasise by contrast the way in which, in *In Memoriam*, the human spirit is still asserting itself against time and space, doubt and despair. It is a historical document from a time when the odds against man were heavy but not overwhelming. The artist still had 'a conscience and an aim', wanting to teach because his readers wanted to learn. Though enmeshed in a new complex of scientific data Tennyson could still, without either ignoring or being ignorant of these data, speculate on man's spiritual nature with something of the old traditional grandeur. Our own age is overwhelmed with data which seem beyond assimilation and impossible to ignore. Tennyson is, if we like, the last great poet to link those soon to be notorious two cultures which now threaten to diminish the stature of man.

For Further Reading

My references to Tennyson's works are to the Macmillan Collected Edition. On the whole, students have been better served by the poet's biographers than by his critics. The *Memoir* by the poet's son Hallam Tennyson (published in one volume by Macmillan, 1899) is essential reading. H. D. Rawnsley's *Memories of the Tennysons* (MacLehose, Glasgow, 1900) is also worth consulting. R. W. Rader's *Tennyson's Maud: the Autobiographical Genesis* (Cambridge, for University of California, 1963) throws some fresh light on Tennyson's state of mind in the years after Hallam's death. Sir Harold Nicolson's *Tennyson* (Constable, 1923; Grey Arrow paperback, 1960) remains the most useful introduction, though I do not agree with all its critical judgements. *Critical Essays on the Poetry of Tennyson*, edited by John Killham (Routledge, 1960) is a collection by various hands and of varying merit: it contains T. S. Eliot's famous essay on *In Memoriam*. Basil Willey's *More Nineteenth Century Studies* (Chatto and Windus, 1956) provides some useful information about Tennyson's philosophical ideas. Finally, A. C. Bradley's exhaustive *Commentary on In Memoriam* (Macmillan, 1901) contains one or two errors and may seem rather old-fashioned in its approach: but it remains a monument to the industry and piety of a major critic.

The standard biography of the poet is by Sir Charles Tennyson (1949). The standard edition of the *Works* is now that edited by C. Ricks (Longmans, 1969).

Index